JET FUMES

JET DRUMHELLER

Jet Fumes

MILTON & HUGO L.L.C.
4407 Park Ave., Suite 5
Union City, NJ 07087, USA

Website: *www. miltonandhugo.com*
Hotline: *1- 888-778-0033*
Email: *info@miltonandhugo.com*

Ordering Information:
Quantity sales. Special discounts are granted to corporations, associations, and other organizations. For more information on these discounts, please reach out to the publisher using the contact information provided above.

Library of Congress Control Number:		2025915620
ISBN-13:	979-8-89285-579-2	[Paperback Edition]
	979-8-89285-580-8	[Digital Edition]

Rev. date: 07/09/2025

DEDICATION

This is dedicated to my wife, who shared many adventures with me along with life in general. She supported this manuscript, offering input at the beginning, but sadly she passed before the conclusion. I believe we'll see each other again in due time.

SPECIAL THANKS

To God and my worn-out guardian angel.

To Emma Lopez, *for* your guidance and insight.

To all those who held me up, pulled me through, and created some unforgettable memories.

And most especially, Mom—and she knows not to read it!

CONTENTS

PARDON THE INTRODUCTION

This is the true story of a life lived by a somewhat inept person fortunate enough to speak of it now. A life of uncertainty, questionable decisions, foolish behavior and extreme activities. 50 plus years of crazy living, 30 plus years in bands, 30 days in rehab, 20 whole minutes to relapse, 10 times waking to question my location and zero self-control. To say I had a fall from grace would be totally inaccurate for two reasons. First, that saying implies I had grace at some point, I did not. Secondly there was no fall, it was more of a cannonball.

The results or consequences of living like a heathen at times are clearly evident to myself and the few others left that agreed certain things should somehow be documented. I have very fond memories of many things, pictures and momentos that bring a smile at times. On the other hand I have flashbacks of some things that can't be undone, and reminders of those as well. Arrest reports, a few scars and my physical being, aching most days. As someone said before no man is an island, if I were an island however I'd be along the lines of Easter Island, strange, inexplicable, hard to reach.

As I began to gather the sordid recollections of times past and started to begin this project there were many pointers as to how to proceed. I was in my very early years a walking migraine, or rough around the edges some might say. It became important to me that the following conveyed the same. The few people I approached to get thoughts from, those with direct knowledge, agreed. What follows is at times itself unpolished to a degree, raw in a few places I suppose. I did believe and still do it is the best approach, the best way to deliver the realities, emotions and express situations. Some language or descriptions of things may seem unnecessary to those unaccustomed to such, I took those things into consideration. Lessening certain language or cleaning up the narratives would not serve the purpose of trying to convey things as they were, or emotions as they were. I never intended to pen a Disney type manuscript. Following some advice from one much better qualified than myself I have lessened the tone in areas.

There was never an intention to be considered for any grammatical or editorial praise. I can imagine some critics pointing to this and that as the work of a novice, and that would be correct. However, it is a section of my life and only I can speak on it. Simply put it is what it is and the final draft conveys what it was, knowingly unperfect.

There were times in my earliest years when some others probably thought I had some brain damage or perhaps might be fitted for a strait jacket. There may be a small degree of truth to the brain question I admit. As for the jacket, if it were a soft leather I'd give it a try. I am not a stupid person by any means, foolish is a much better description. I know a little about a lot of things and I know a lot about a few things. Other than foolish I have also been extremely compulsive, to the point of far beyond what might be considered normal.

I understand now compulsiveness and foolishness go hand in hand and mirror each other a bit. When combined as part of a person's actual being it's not a good match. The compulsive issue for me was ever present and it took very little to rouse it. A simple sight, smell, random thought, billboard, a dare or challenge, to name a few triggers. If I wanted to see, feel, experience, calm any curiosity I just went with the thought as if I were robotic. I and others as well suffered a lot of consequences as a result. Then the foolishness kicked in as if jealous, meaning whatever I had done I would simply repeat. Not the actual act that was in question at the time, although it did occur, more of the lack of common sense. Maybe a later time in a different setting but obviously a repeat. We live and learn however, I only acted that way 49 years.

Not all but most of my misadventures were accompanied by like-minded cohorts, partners in crime and the like either clearing my path, leading, following or encouraging my idiocy with phrases like "I dare you", or "what's the matter, you scared,"? and the ever powerful "I got your back, go ahead". I dare say each and every one has heard at some point the two fatal phrases, "I promise" and "you can trust me." Upon hearing things like that the first time and maybe even the second, I felt comfortable enough to carry on with my little secret or scheme. Those individuals were rooted out but did leave a hard learned lesson.

I blame no one really, sometimes situations arise that impact people simply by virtue of being in any particular place at the exact moment something occurred. Life itself does confront people with choices and the following decisions made usually dictate some type of lesson, sooner or later. There are some, like myself, that just didn't accept some lessons. There were things done or said in my presence however that I wish hadn't occurred, or reactions that followed. The right place-right time scenario has a nemesis as do all things, wrong place-wrong time.

When the ingredients that made my life were all mixed however it formed a life about as fucked up as a football bat. I guess most would refer to this as a memoir, as I proceeded however I wondered if there was such a thing as a forgetmoir. What follows is an account of things I saw, did, experienced and/or felt. Every single incident or mishap I was involved in would be entirely too much to get into, I just focused on a small portion of things that in some cases might be better ignored and buried. I had to be reminded of several instances either by word of mouth or visible marks and decided to narrow things down quite a bit as the memories were mostly unpleasant. There were actually more good memories by comparison that I am reminded of unexpectedly but the bad ones always outweighed the good, not in quantity but quality. I suppose a scar or broken bone was more memorable than a walk through the park.

My intention is that this release may be therapeutic for me and perhaps a warning of sorts for others, a kind of accounting. I have been pulled through, rescued, fortunate and otherwise simply blessed to still be present and able to attempt this writing on things normally better left unsaid. Every aspect of my life was not a complete train wreck, but at times there were no tracks, no engineer, maybe a bridge or 2 missing. On that matter, yes it is hard to stop a train.

As a backdrop I have always loved the arts and the creativity they promote. That should say enough in itself, the artsy type, or better yet a musician. Throughout life I have drawn, painted, written, sculpted, studied the martial arts and performed but the biggest passion by far was music. I feel it, swim in it, certainly done my share of playing. Song structure, bridges, an ear for misplaced notes or chords, lyrics and what they meant somehow just came naturally to me. I did have to learn things on my own from others but there is just something internally with most musicians.

I had experimented briefly with guitars and the piano but my calling was percussion. I suppose it was always my interest in using my hands, letting them speak for me either on canvas, a drum set, self-defense courses or anything of the sort. I have had the pleasure that comes in the roles of a husband, father, grandfather, father figure, care giver and occasionally teacher. Those all came to me early in my life, I haven't reached 60 at this point. I suppose it would be a blessing if that birthday comes.

I had other roles as well that were not quite as glamorous. Class clown, trouble maker, dumbass, idiot. I guess I took those roles just as seriously as the others. They say if you're going to do something do it right. Why be sent to the principal's office for being a simple every day class clown when I could be Bozo? Likewise, if I'm going to be called a dumbass I would strive to be the dumbest ass.

I never really had a whole lot to offer the world in terms of eye opening inspiration or scientific breakthroughs so I did what I could with what little I had to offer. As I thought about that I realized there were breakthroughs by people at certain points in time that were praised by many, cursed just the same. The great Archimedes certainly is associated with a large influence on math as it is practiced today, damn him. The one who envisioned the mini skirt and brought it to life didn't get the same praise although they are of equal genius. Those comparisons represent what I brought to the table of life.

What talents and interests I did have I did my best to study, learn and understand as much as possible. Those efforts mostly paid off in one way or another, but some of those interests were not exactly the kind of things to talk to mom about. I still threw all the effort I could into them right or wrong. If I offer nothing else I could always be a good bad example!

On a more intellectual level I have been known to say things that just rubbed others the wrong way, at times purposely. Inappropriate, rude, out of place, cruel or mean. The following material will in some cases bear that out depending on the individual reader. Please allow me to address that from the beginning, hopefully gathering a little understanding.

It is very true that at times my mouth had gotten ahead of my brain, or more eloquently put, my mouth had written a check my ass couldn't cash. There were times I said things I wish I hadn't, times I spoke out of anger or emotions which indeed hurt some, at times to the point of crying. I do admit those mistakes, there were outcomes that I regret and I have apologized, I felt the pain also.

Those issues were typically in a private setting or a situation otherwise not public. On the other side I have said or implied things not out of rudeness or indifference but simply because it was truth. I am not and have never been accused of being politically correct. I don't believe in that notion unless one is trying to land a job or run a scam. Other than that if a person is an asshole just say "you're a real asshole." Don't go buy a sweet Hallmark card and a book on etiquette. If there was a book available entitled 'Etiquette for Assholes' maybe. Nahh.

In those circumstances where truth was spoken and feelings hurt, truth being the operative word, the circumstance then becomes about feelings and/or that person facing the truth. Why spend 25 minutes protecting someone's ego when 3 minutes can say it all?

This topic is one where I believe society has failed, things were better years ago when a person could speak their mind, call a spade a spade without worry of bullshit lawsuits, and there were no lingering questions like "what are you saying?" Just cut to the chase, speak the truth and be done.

If actual truth hurts feelings, feelings should be addressed, not truth. That type of thing is important when one is trying to avoid trouble with authorities or perhaps clear their own name, perhaps get a date.

Over some time it had been suggested to me to visit with therapists so that I might be pointed in the right direction. This manuscript is the result of one such meeting, her thought being it may be beneficial for me to take responsibility, admitting and accepting things and releasing some pressure. It has been helpful I will say to just let go, be open and tell it like it is, or was. Internally a volcano begins to form shame, guilt, worry or embarrassment. In that regard I give credit where and when due. The very large majority of other therapists I had seen were to me useless. Mostly degrading, holier than thou, even resorting to name calling on one occasion. Thankfully I met and spoke with one finally who was open and polite, she made me realize there was and still remains much to expel, there is no joy in feeling like a pimple on the ass of life. It didn't hurt any that she had a great personality, well spoken, ruby red nails and form fitting attire. She also had some document in a frame that eluded to her being able to do stuff like talking about things, acting interested and giving the impression she had years of knowledge concerning the intricacies of human nature. All of those attributes by the age of no more than 25. I guess it was the nails and clothes that got me.

STAGE I

Allow me to formally introduce myself, my name is Jet. I do realize the oddity of the name but I assure you I've been called much worse. How such a name came about is really unimportant but it is truly music to my ears in comparison to some other names I've been called combined with poignant adjectives.

Concerning my introduction to the world, I suppose it must have been bittersweet, sweet to my mother but bitter to others. It's almost as if I remember hearing "uuugghhh" upon my initial appearance, followed by the sight of the one who had yanked me from my existence. How dare this person touch my baby soft baby ass and hold me by my ankle upside down like I was a banana or up for some kind of auction. I had just been kicked out of the only existence I knew only to be greeted by some monster who couldn't pass me off quick enough to another that looked like a worn out shoe, but the touch and feeling was unmistakeable, my poor ole worn out mom.

As a child I used to think my name was Jesus Christ, and I mean no offense by that, it's just all I vaguely remember hearing.... "Jesus Christ what did you do"? or "Jesus Christ that's not a toy" as I was playing in the tub with an absence of actual toys, I guess I was playing with something. Apparently I was instilled with a strong sense of adventure at birth. My mom would tell me later that one particular day I was in my crib sleeping, so she thought, and after some time she came to check on me as things were strangely quiet. Much to her surprise I wasn't there or anywhere else to be found. It didn't take her long to look seeing as how our house had wheels on it, very small. In her panic she glanced at the door and noticed it slightly opened. That discovery was odd enough by itself, it had snowed several inches and the door should be closed. As she investigated further she was greeted by a tiny little trail that led down a couple of cinderblocks, steps if you prefer, and on out through the yard. Eventually I was located maybe 30 yards away at a little paved play area with a few neighborhood kids who obviously were somewhat older. I suppose I'd heard them playing and I hadn't received an invitation which provoked me.

She never could figure how I got out of the crib or through the door. The thought then turned to why did I not appear to be cold or even care about the snow. It remains a mystery still and was just the beginning. The snow may have been a blessing because the closer she got that brown diaper must have really stood out in the pristine snow. It wasn't brown when she put it on but hey, that's what it's for.

I pulled the same stunt in first grade with the exception being I was obviously older and had at least some thought process. I asked to be excused from class and on my trip to the bathroom I decided I was just plain bored and the weather looked pleasant. Out the door, down the steps and running hard. When I got winded I stopped at some old closed down building and crawled under the entry stairs to formulate my next move. Little did I know calls were being made, people freaking out everywhere, police now involved. Well I somehow made it to my grannies house but was beaten there by the authorities. There was crying and hugging and much relief, not from the ones in uniform, followed by the demands that I explain my actions and how serious things had become. I don't remember any particular reason other than the opportunity was there. My first run in with the law.

In my single digit years there were new brilliant shows such as Star Trek, Batman, Bewitched. I do believe Samantha the witch was my first little crush. Over the airwaves were the Stones, the Doors and of course the Beatles were established firmly. Sinatra, Capt. Kangaroo and unknown to many, H R PuffnStuff. My God how bizarre! Witchypoo, a talking flute, some kind of perverted pumpkin head freak pedophile thing, wow. Plain to see drug testing was not yet in effect.

As mentioned earlier I was always an artsy type, always had that type of mindset and it paid off occasionally though not to an occupational degree. I didn't depend on those interests for serious income, there were normal jobs, 2 of which were highly regulated and required a high degree of specific training and perpetual oversight. I performed well and the work was respectable but at the same time any little mistake could be disastrous which was the cause of too much stress. The occupations were obviously necessary but never diminished my interests otherwise. There were things to consider when entering into the workplace after all, income, respectability, at times insurance, and the need to fund those other interests.

While navigating through this life I did indeed see and do many things, a lot of which were illegal, immoral or just not acceptable in society. The question becomes exactly who determines what's unacceptable? Of course the laws and those enforcing them are excluded, but we do certainly have those who are very anxious to dictate their views of right and wrong. As impressionable as small children are it is imperative that those in any teaching capacity choose their words carefully. I for one had visions of burning alive, suffering endlessly because I was a sinner yet at my age I couldn't figure out what I'd done.

Some fire and brimstone preacher convinced me of it and for some time I was scared to death. A kid can only comprehend so much. I don't wish that on anyone, just saying.

Most memories I now have of those days were re-gifted to me courtesy of my big sis, one of which was myself as the great "Underwear Man". Apparently I would use a towel or anything I could to replicate a cape around my neck as I ran around in my underwear seeking and destroying any living thing that wanted nothing more than to be left alone. Underwear Man couldn't have that! I fed off of her disgust and efforts to keep me contained like a crazed baboon. There is no denying we fought each other physically and mentally through the early years but in the end made us both stronger and tolerant.

One could say I was a problem child and to some degree still exhibit similar behavior. Why let little things like age or adulthood get in the way? Responsibility? Who the hell wants that? Whenever something is wrong one of the first questions is "who's responsible for this?" Nobody needs that kind of pressure. The 'act your age' thing I get to some degree, but there are areas where from my point of view, it just doesn't apply. I see people my age acting their age everywhere I go. Falling asleep in front of the TV at 5:00 pm, driving 35 mph in a 60 mph zone, holding up 8 people in line at a grocery checkout while searching for a 50 cents off coupon, and the worst...once that coupon is found and redeemed, only then dig around in their fanny pack trying to locate an actual check book which of course means writing. Writing requires a pen which now must be found. Upon finding it, the block letter writing begins only to be interrupted by the need to ask the date and double check the amount. The same steps repeat as that information now must go into the register of the checkbook, and finally study the receipt, letter by letter, and top to bottom. God forbid that person makes an error while filling out the check and has to void it, only to start again. Each to his own, maybe I'll get there one day, if someone drags me kicking and screaming. Either way there is a light at the end of the tunnel as they say. I can imagine in some cases that light being shined by some paramedic into one's eyes while searching for a pulse. It makes more sense I suppose to return to the beginning.

I do know factually for a very brief time I was the youngest person on the planet, my one claim to fame. When asked what state I was born in I just reply "what state? Same as everybody else, slimy and screaming like hell". Let's just say I'm close to the border.

I fondly do remember my mom and sister, who was 2 years older at the time, and did remain 2 years older from then on I suppose. They both had a big role in my life, from mom teaching and preaching and loving and whipping my ass as needed, to big sis who just whipped my ass for no apparent reason without the teaching. My grandparents, long passed, spent quality time with me as they could. As for my grandpop the quality might have been in question. He asked me once, only once, to be his assistant painting chairs or something like that. My little creative mind somehow thought that the cat would look better white and so my artistry went to work. The cat was not cooperative as one would expect and thankfully rescued before a second coat was applied. I suppose it was beneficial for all he didn't ask me to help carve a pumpkin.

Moving on my sis frequently complained I was always messing around in her room, going through her shit. Well at least that's what her diary said. She carried on at times about some crazy girl named Mary who apparently was quite popular and was the life of the party, Mary Jane I believe she was referred to. I thought it strange I knew nothing of her being my sis was so enamored with her. When I did meet Mary, unavoidable, she proved to be very alluring, captivating me and screwed me without mercy. If that wasn't enough her cousins were waiting in the wings and I likewise welcomed them also. It's been portrayed many times if a person welcomes a vampire into a dwelling the seal is broken, the vampire waltzes right in, appearing in whatever form the other wants to see. It's brilliant honestly in a deceptive manner and my door was no more than the type one would expect to see in a saloon.

As important as the bonds were between the 3 of us there was another strange unexplainable presence with me or around me at all times and remains to the day. I would have to say a guardian angel for lack of knowledge otherwise. Nothing maleficent in my view, fact is I don't know and really don't care for it, not a real big fan of the unseen. What I do know is there was a watch over me for as far back as I can remember. I could sense or feel things out of nowhere, in any given circumstance although I was alone. I knew eyes were on me at times, even worse the overwhelming feeling of not being alone, to the point of touch almost. That sort of knowing something never left and remains still, especially considering several "close calls" I've had over time but pulled through, or perhaps was pulled through.

I still clearly recall something audibly walking through the kitchen and the 6 feet or so it took to get to open door of my room. I wasn't any more than 5 or 6, everybody was in bed so there was no reason to be hearing that, and no one to account for it. I threw my covers over my head and other than shaking was motionless, petrified. At my door was who knows what, after clearly having made that trek which I undoubtedly heard. I don't know if it came into the room or just stopped and stared or what but even now there is no doubt whatsoever. My memory is subject at times but there are things branded, tattooed. That wasn't the end of that type of thing but I don't speak on it much.

Much further along in age I did truly have insights, visions, dreams, whatever description fits. I don't know how they formed or how they got to me, very confusing. At some point I began to have tiny morsels of memories of my childhood and I realized I'd had the same thing happen at times then. At a much younger age I paid them no mind, decades later it's easier to grasp I suppose.

Several of those instances were bizarre in that I just knew I'd seen some particular place or person before, or had already heard what I was now hearing. Many times some obscure song would pop into my head as I was getting ready or cleaning. Not your average top 40 song but one from 30 years ago that wasn't even top 40 then, maybe aired 4 times in a year. I finish whatever I'm doing, get in the car to run an errand and that song is immediately playing. Once or twice is one thing, but over and over makes me curious.

The two biggest eye openers by far, I had seen the events of 9-11-2001 beforehand and the Covid crisis as well. The problem was or is I didn't know how to decipher what was popping into my head. I didn't see the actual skyscrapers or planes, I saw something specific in flight, I don't want to go into detail, spewing out some type of acidic poison that would dissolve anything it came into contact with. There were several of these objects each doing the same causing massive destruction, screaming and panic. I was in some vehicle which likewise had been sprayed and the windows began to more or less melt. I remember being very upset, half scared really, then it was over. It took a little while to put it behind me, then the actual event happened and it all came back.

With the COVID situation I remember something reminiscent of a cloud, something cloud like. Dark, barely translucent, shifting and moving quickly in different directions as if by its own will. The best description I guess is visualizing a swarm of locusts from afar. Something was being emitted in the form of a fog or mist, not quite sure. The main thing I vividly recall is a giant black bat, wings spread out fully, the two were simultaneous. Not long after COVID hit, again bringing those sights back to me, and shortly thereafter came the bat theory.

On those two occasions my mind briefly erased those little dreams but they came storming back when reality hit. Also, in both cases I had not and could not decipher what I'd experienced, I know each time I was very uneasy afterwards and tucked them away. In no way am I saying I have some unique ability or anything of the sort. I just know that it happened, it was all confusing and misunderstood by me. I spoke to maybe 2 trusted people about it, along with a few other occurrences and just asked that it remain private.

More than likely we all have those experiences at times, some just don't realize it or choose to ignore. I know now that things of that nature do happen, and not in association with some deck of cards or trance like state. It comes when it comes.

Speaking of things invisible or unknown, that's probably the best description of my father. I never met the guy. I don't recall ever really knowing I was missing something then but it would bite me in the ass later, many times. I only heard a whisper here and there of his existence throughout the years and it was made clear that I should never ask, wonder, anything. So, that only deepened my curiosity. Who the hell was this guy? Where did he go and why? Has he ever tried to contact me without my knowledge? Is it possible I have brothers or other sisters? Even worse, did he do something to me that others were hiding? I never got any satisfactory information so it remains unknown. All I have is my birth certificate bearing his name which only serves as proof that he could father a child and nothing more. Curiosity still gets the best of me occasionally.

I must admit I never realized our financial situation simply because our neighbors were just as bad off. In short we were poor. Oddly enough we were considered the upper class of the area because our home had snow tires, not cheap shit! It was really unfair to have that well to do sin cast upon us, its equivalent to comparing the broken down cars in each others' yards. One might be a 1976 pinto station wagon, the other some ford pickup minus the bed and mismatched doors, but the pinto rests on cinderblocks whereas the truck is elevated by a jack. The rumors circulate as to how could they afford a jack? I've seen the very wealthy do the same with other wealthy people, human nature I suppose.

Mom did everything humanly possible and then some but how much could a single young mother do in those days? When we sat down at our kitchen table for dinner our elbows were in the living room. The insurance premium was probably based on those beautiful snow tires and wheels the house had attached to it. We did not have money, but our mom made us not realize or care. Things certainly could have been worse. Likewise there was no understanding of with or without because everyone was without. If you're driving 100 mph and everyone else is also you don't notice. We had much love and support, as much as a single hard working mom could give plus a little bit more. So loving, comforting, dedicated and by the way about as devout a Christian as one could ever meet. Sis and I would not latch onto that anchor for some time. I'll finish by saying she never once waivered in her faith or love for us, something that we didn't appreciate fully for years.

I don't know how or when it happened but sometime during my dirty diaper days mom met this man who would eventually become my dad or better put my father figure. I never could or did call him dad. Scott was a manly man, tall and broad, well built, polite and very much covered with hair. At first I thought he might be a gorilla wearing a tank top yet could talk. He became a regular presence to our delight and what a blessing he was. My first and last most influential male figure, no longer just the skirts and me.

We played and roughhoused as they say, something I hadn't been accustomed to. He was my new buddy, playmate and a man, whereas before there was none. Good times.

By virtue of him simply being there I was able to participate in things other kids take for granted, including having the actual father around. We would go camping, canoeing, sledding, all the things that would have never happened without Scott. That being said he was definitely not interested in any type of sports activities, hunting or fishing. He was the type that had he been stung by a scorpion he would get a box and somehow get it inside, get it to the porch and relocate it to it's new home, some old dirty aquarium he never discarded and now filled with sand and vegetables and a little scorpion bed. I'd seen him go into action with mice myself, a mousetrap was not an option. Gather them up, again somehow in a box and release them somewhere outside to which they thought "why does he keep doing this", and they made their way back just before nightfall.

When I thought things couldn't get better I was introduced to Scott the musician and life took on a new meaning. This discovery, this new world would prove to be a life changing event, one of several. These events and others would go into my "Soul Box".

Scott it turns out was a drummer, practicing and playing this whole time unbeknownst to me. At some point it was determined that I could accompany him to practice and I suppose I didn't really have other obligations. From the very instant I walked into that garage I would never be the same. The drum set, lights, amps, guitars, unbelievable. Then the actual sound, oh man a cymbal does that?? That guitar did what?? I saw their brotherhood, how close they were and the mutual respect...shaking their heads as they played, tapping their feet...and bigfoot on the drums! I was in awe and have never looked back. I have often felt sorry for those who had or have no musical background. It's very involved with the beat and count, the meaning and love, expressions, feelings. So yes it changed me then and unto this very day.

I look back at some of the many live shows I've seen, the parts I do remember, and I didn't fully appreciate the magnitude at the time. The Who, Elton John, U2, Van Halen x 4, Aerosmith, Stevie Nicks, INXS, KISS, only to name a few. Acts that cannot be seen again. I always enjoyed a good stage performance regarding some excitement and a heartfelt effort to get the audience involved in the whole affair.

There are things that are just embedded, born into our individual being, some say human nature. A feel for some type of beat or tempo, something not created in nature itself but felt internally. Every continent and culture had its own unique instruments and interpretations of what sound pleased them, going back well before any written language. Of course there are other traits instilled, the need to raid and conquer, perpetual war waging, racism, dishonesty. Music however is the one that people use to share their thoughts on the other traits. In the long run the pictures are much easier on the eyes also. My curiosity is who and why someone at some point thought... what if we kill that animal over there, slice the skin off, let it bake in the sun for a few days and, oh I don't know, stretch it across some logs and beat it with leg bones. What's the worst that could happen?

Next thing you know the very first groupie was making her moves, proudly pulling that beaver ribcage through her beautiful unibrow, making sure her hair was free of mosquitos and such, fresh coconut half shells on each breast and even brushed her tooth. Well even back then men were assholes. They beat their rocks and logs, threw her over their humpbacks and dragged her to the nearest cave only to fall asleep.

As I moved on in my bizarre world I'm not exactly a baby anymore but I did require oversight while the adults were away and sis joined me briefly. Enter the babysitter. This young lady was apparently an acquaintance of my mom but I can't say how. Very slender, tall, hair past her waist and unmistakable round hippy glasses...it was more than just a look, hippy all the way. Not like the wannabees today, the genuine thing.

The scenery was a little strange to me at that time. I recall lots of beads, candles, very vivid colors and her oversized flowing clothes. Our principle area of existence was the basement of some house, I do remember stairs that led to an unwelcoming dimly lit basement. The set up was such that in the minds of my sis and I a monster could lurk anywhere. As long as the sitter was present everything was ok but she had other obligations at times.

I am unable to say what happened or why but several times sis and I would be punished(?) meaning sent to the place we feared most. I do recall the 2 of us huddled together on the top step pressed to the door, crying and scared to death. As if that were not enough it happened on an individual basis as well. Clearly we were heard crying out but were ignored. As evident it was not forgotten. When I see or hear about someone I love having been hurt my empathy is overwhelming, matched by anger on the opposite end. We both had to be spanked, disciplined as needed in our very young lives, a practice that has faded over the years along with manners and morals. Hearing sis go through it made me angry, sometimes a nervous wreck. By the way, that whole "go outside and get a big switch so I can whip your ass" thing was psychological torture. It's like you're gonna set me on fire but I have to get the matches?? In other words you have enough energy to spank me but too damn lazy to get the job done without getting off your ass? Followed by the assumption you had taught a lesson. You actually did, more than you know. The babysitter herself wasn't involved as I recall, her mother was the culprit.

During my stays there the love of music was undeniable. The Beatles, Three Dog Night, The Doors. I'd be willing to bet I knew every word, every note to the entire Sgt. Pepper's album start to finish within 3 months. By this time my thirst for music and the knowledge thereof had magnified. At that very young age I'm trying to decipher the deepest lyrics of McCartney, Lennon, Morrison and the like. Much too young for that but there were no cell phones, cable, internet or video games. My imaginary friend went to play with an imaginary kid and never came back so you do what you have to.

She was a smoker but it was of no consequence at the time. One day however, while sitting with mom in a restaurant and observing a couple smoking it hit me...those people are doing something very different then what I witness at the babysitters. There's no bubbling sound, they're not lighting it every two minutes, and they blow out the smoke right away. Hmmm..

Well long story short I had to inquire during my next stay and she was not hesitant to educate me. She explained this device and the purpose of it, most importantly the ingredient that made it actually work. Eventually she handed it to me and in my nervous excitement I turned it up as if to drink the water. She caught me quickly but I did manage to get a tiny taste, believe me I only did that once. That lesson being learned, I became a quick study in the proper use of that device and the contents thereof. I don't believe she meant any harm at all, but it was a bad decision. I never looked back.

As she continued to watch over me so to speak, I was ingesting just a little bit more here and there and I guess thinking this is normal. It's a good assumption I think that my mind at that age never gave things a second thought. The magic device is used when you're happy, when you're sad, bored or having fun, any time of day or night. What follows is pretty obvious, can't do without it. In that regard it was a life changing slow going issue, and another right behind.

One day while sitting, sunning in a neighbors' yard I noticed there was a large dog running around and enjoying life, so why not go play. I threw sticks and balls which he would fetch and bring back like a never ending game. At some point something happened, something very wrong. The dog and I were facing each other maybe fifteen yards apart and suddenly it looked at me, as if uncertain about something, it slowly turned its head to one side and all hell broke loose.

This beast just took off in my direction and was at me before I could blink or think. It leaped from maybe four yards away and hit me like a damn cannonball. Thinking back it was just as big or bigger than me. Before I could comprehend, think, react or anything I was under attack. As a visual, this dog was a full grown German Shepard, very large and as I would know later prone to bad behavior. I vaguely recall overhearing that it had bitten or tried to attack others here and there, this house was his second or third.

I learned extremely quickly true fear, panic and helplessness, then real physical pain. Throughout life we all experience these things surely, but all at the same time?

All I really remember is that look, that head turning, that mouth opening and fangs. It was almost as if I was wearing a sausage necklace and bacon earrings. I can just recall the biting and scratching and its head going side to side, but just as horrific for me was the sound it made. A low throaty growl with sudden barks. I have no idea how long it lasted, I think I blacked out or whatever a panicked kid does. I do know it took two people to pull it off and escort it inside. For a moment I was left sprawled out in the yard screaming, bite marks, scratched, a little bloody and petrified. I was taken inside and had some first aid treatments applied which was probably just an attempt to calm me. I needed a lot more than cream or bandages, I just didn't realize it. That is where memory quit.

That experience left me changed and I knew it was a close call. There were other actions to follow that were questionable to say the least, and almost as harmful. First, it was made somewhat clear that it was just unfortunate, dogs sometimes do that. "Oh it's not that bad, you'll be okay. Let's get something to drink." Meanwhile Cujo is getting his belly rubbed and being scolded with baby talk.

What doesn't kill you makes you stronger! Yeah I'm gonna have to call bullshit on that. How about if I accidentally dropped a giant hornets nest in the bathroom floor while someone was showering and closed the door. Once the screaming is done and the person is removed by paramedics suddenly they're stronger? I realize it refers to a mental state but still, no. That was adult shit trying to cover their asses because they did not control an unleashed aggressive beast. In the end, no need to talk about it again, that was my impression. I could never ever forget.

I think it's important to mention as well that in those days and in that particular place there were no leash laws. A majority of neighbors had dogs, some had 2 or 3. Just about every day as I was walking the street or even going to the mailbox 1 or 2 dogs would approach me, some running, others with a fast walk, looking directly at me. In most cases they were big and barking or growling. If I were riding my bike it was far worse. That was an invitation to chase full speed and attack my legs or at least rip my pants to shreds. At times I just wouldn't go out.

PTSD is something mostly associated with the military but there are other applications as well. It was traumatic and I certainly gained a disorder. Absolutely no offense to any armed forces, I served myself.

Following that particular incident there was yet another situation concerning another dog, somewhat similar to the first one but the conclusion was very different. One afternoon while strolling around I saw a dog going after a kitten, tiny little thing you could hold in your hand. The helpless thing was no match, caught quickly in the dog's mouth and destroyed in front of my eyes as I yelled for help. Just know it did not survive. For the second time I had seen the evil deeds of dogs, but this time I vowed to hunt that animal down and hurt it just as I and the kitten had been. After looking from house to house I found him, sitting by the porch as if all was well, but all was not well indeed. With my pipe in my little hand I slowly approached intent on killing him right in his own yard, and he saw me coming.

We locked eyes seemingly forever as I inched closer, now shaking a little and nervous about what I was about to do. He sat up on his butt, tongue hanging out with the appearance of wanting to play or something. At that very moment a voice came into my mind, into my soul, along with a comfort or peace I hadn't known before....

"Do not harm this animal, he has done no wrong. He does not reason... you want to hurt because you are hurt."

I did walk away thank God, and cried my eyes out. The vision of what happened to that little kitten had struck a painful flashback in me, I didn't or couldn't understand at the time but that inner voice was unmistakable. I had to accept that whatever the dog had done was natural to him, nothing evil. Later it did occur to me that I alone had to be in that exact place on that particular day at that exact moment in order to witness or perhaps learn. If I had so much as stubbed a toe beforehand and had to recover for 1 minute it would have never come to pass.

I do know now and have for some time how very special dogs are, truly gifts to most people, furry little kids and a best friend without question. I have owned several that I worshipped to death, but they were on the small side.

As is the case life moves on, we moved to a location maybe 10 minutes away on the clock but worlds away in my reality. It only makes sense that heads of the household hoped and wished for aesthetics in life, of course I never knew then moving was even an option. When sis and I saw the inside it was as if we'd hit the lottery. A hallway was a nice addition, before there had only been more of a way. There were defined areas, as in the kitchen and living room had separation by virtue of a doorway. In the other place one could get a drink, fix a bowl of ice cream, grab a napkin, adjust the coat hanger antenna on the TV and answer the door all without leaving the plastic lounge chair.

The most significant change for us kids were private rooms, the size or layout did not matter. It was especially important to sis after the complete lack of privacy and peace I had bestowed upon her. The yard was yet another blessing, we now had available distance between us to throw a frisbee or play catch. Previously we just handed the frisbee off to each other. In the event someone actually threw it we just watched it sail away, hoping the new owners would enjoy it.

In the interim Scott had presented me with my first little drum set and I walled everything else out. At maybe 10 or 11 I was in my first band and it was an awesome feeling, quite sure the music was far from enjoyable to any souls within listening distance. After some much needed practice and with some parental help we had our first shot at performing live at a facility that housed and cared for mentally unstable people, some a little unpredictable. This engagement also just happened to be on a Halloween night, no joking. For the life of me I can't remember how it came about or whose bright idea it was but the "show" did go on.

We were kids and excited as could be, there were no inclinations or thoughts of why we probably shouldn't do it. As we were being parentally driven into the packed arena feeling like rock stars our excitement was tamed somewhat as we started to be educated in the fact that some people are just different.

Try to imagine about 200 or so mentally challenged people, dressed up for Halloween, watching a live band be it kids or not. God bless them, they were having a sort of outing, dancing and such, enjoying the sights and sounds and that honestly warmed my heart, the visual is impossible to explain. They were clapping and hugging us when we finished, and what did my dumb ass decide to do? Well as an excited kid drummer I started handing out drumsticks! How did that work out? Let me preach on it. By the time we left they were beating every damn thing in sight to death whether it was glass, doors or furniture, no matter to them. Some were leaning out of windows half naked singing just as loud as they could and the staff was somewhat overwhelmed I recall. Try to imagine Charles Manson after 4 coffees and a donut, given 2 wooden sticks, on Halloween no less, multiply that by 100. I can't help but grin when I imagine if we had set off pyrotechnics or God forbid incorporated strobe lights.

Someone trying to do something good for us kids had been in agreement with another at that facility that the whole thing was such a good idea for all. Really? How about during their break we have them shooting apples out of each other's mouths with arrows filled with sulfuric acid?? It truly is amazing how things did not turn out absolutely horrendous all things considered. My heart goes out to those having to live life in such an atmosphere because I know full well they did not choose it for themselves. Those who care for them are simply amazing. I personally am responsible for ensuring they earned their pay that night. Pretty damn sure it remains a one-time thing.

Moving on, with this drum set and new neighborhood, everything is coming together....as in the perfect storm. Trying to discern why or how we managed to find or create trouble so easily is complicated, rest assured we were responsible for 90%. There were factors that inadvertently helped along the way when the big picture is taken in. Consider please, in my pre-teen years and for years that followed life was much different. We didn't have the electronics and other luxuries that are considered part of everyday life today. For quite some time no cable TV either. If we were watching one of the three channels available and decided to watch something else we actually had to, get this, get up, walk to the TV and manually change the channel. For some today that's hard to fathom. Kids went outside most of the time to be together in person as opposed to a tiny screen. Things were said face to face, no hiding behind a phone or the like. That in itself could spawn trouble but if so it was handled then, not carried on for days through texting. Without the modern things of today we had to entertain ourselves and a lot of times use our imagination, again a potential pitfall. Most kids today wouldn't understand jumping a bike over trash cans or climbing trees and playing with broken bottles, maybe rummaging through a dump site. That being said they also don't have the scars or broken bones that go along with those things. Simply put we lived where there was practically nothing available for the young ones to enjoy which left one option, entertain themselves. Idle hands, boredom and drugs are not a good mix.

Our new neighborhood had always been referred to as "across the river" those on the other side should be aware. Be careful when you go across the river, that sort of thing. It was a tough place, not extreme by any means, but edgy, sometimes unforgiving. You stood your ground or got your ass whipped or both. There were a few times when a persons' age or gender did not matter. I had been confronted by young boys twice my age and size, females as well. I can't recall the reasons why but I'm pretty damn sure it was because we just occupied the same space. I may have mouthed off at one point, it's possible.

Two of our neighbors were deaf and dumb though not related. I watched in amazement as their loved ones would use sign language while still showing emotion or emphasis. I had not seen it before and it appeared so odd, simply amazing. To me it was then and is now truly an art, not something simple to decipher however. It just drew me in and I learned what I could in passing. I still do practice it at times using a manual, and in my view it is equal in beauty and style to Egyptian Heiroglyhics, and for some just as difficult to understand. My enjoyment really was knowing they enjoyed just communicating, a gift most people really take for granted. It's painful to imagine someone who could only truly speak to another if the other knew how, I would imagine that percentage rate is extremely low. It was nothing more than average chat, of course I couldn't decipher every single thing but enough to get the point. On the other hand, when one of them got mad or upset about something the best bet was to take a couple of steps back. Their hands and arms not only speak but also show emotion with abrupt moves and such. Anyone within that reach area could have an eye poked or worse, get slapped or scratched. I learned to either duck, dodge or back up. To me it made the whole process even more amazing.

As for those who can verbalize but sometimes shouldn't, our new town had it's share. In one instance some neighborhood punk kid got all up in my face about who knows what and things escalated quickly. I grabbed him, slammed him down but went down also. As I was pummeling him there weren't many choices he could make so in desperation he bit me, took a little chunk out of the chest area. I really didn't feel it at that moment with all the adrenaline I suppose but the pain would certainly come later. I had to have it checked out medically having heard a bite like that from a person was potentially more dangerous than from some animals. It did make me anxious because I knew what had been in the mouths of some others and I'll have to leave that to anyone's imagination.

In the process I learned I had broken his collar bone, very painful. It was then I realized why he bit, as I said he had no choice and could not put up a proper defense. I had no way of knowing what had happened, adrenaline was pumping, others yelling or screaming. I suppose I had knocked the breath out of him when I slammed him very hard to the ground. I tried to imagine such a painful break, can't breathe, can't verbalize anything, still receiving punches. I still have my scar as a reminder and I'm quite sure he remembers as well.

There was, as in most cases, no winner and it was such a relief to realize it's done, over. It ended as it had started, quickly and without understanding.

It's only after the fact you hear maybe it's not quite over. In the coming days I would hear about his big brother or 5 cousins or even his father looking for retribution which occasionally happened. I really felt bad for what had happened and remained on edge for a while.

Following the biting incident and keeping the area in mind there was an instance where myself and another gentleman were trying to gain possession of a knife at the same time. I had grabbed it tight, he did the same but he had the largest part of the handle. He drew back very quickly with force, pulling the knife through my closed hand which did a job on all four fingers and most of the palm. That itself was the factor that decided it was over, and thankfully it was.

There are cases indeed where someone is simply just looking for trouble without reason and typically will find it. Careful what you wish for! I can speak on the matter with clarity, and trouble doesn't always equate to fights, there are limitless types of trouble.

There are times when you just don't care when considering the other participant. One evening some punk kid came up to me at a middle school dance trying to look intimidating and asked if I had danced with his girlfriend which was itself berating. I've seen baby deer on frozen ponds that had better moves than myself. I did have one slow dance attempt with one person so it had to be her. Now immediately I get the clear sensation he wants a fight, over that silly incident. His friends were watching nearby as were others, fully expecting action. I became very angry quickly for a few reasons.

First, the fact he took the time and effort to come to me for such a crazy reason, knowing he had backup and fully expecting me to cave in. Secondly whatever issue may have been swirling in his head would have best been suited to discuss outside. Finally, in my view he intended to use me to solidify his image or perhaps create one. Oh hell no.

I looked him in the eye and said "yeah I danced with her, one dance...that's it, nothing to it". He was completely caught off guard, never thought not only would I admit to it but kind of forcefully admit it. The ball has been slapped hard back into his court. He said "ok, that's what I heard, just wanted to check". He turned and walked away and that was it.

My being honest along with unyielding was the difference. Had I become skiddish, lied about it or shown some nervousness things would have been different. He had not planned for my reaction, therefore had no plan B. As for him, I say if you can't bite don't show your teeth. That being said I'd already been bitten once.

I will say that as I look back we created our own hell in most cases, the name of a town is just a name. This is where my sis and I met and mingled with some real characters, kids who knew things and did things we hadn't seen before, but we learned and adapted. I'd seen actual footage of baby birds barely crawling to the edge of their nest while mom was away and just drop right out. During that quick freefall the wings just came out and they would land on the ground without grace but had learned about those wings. There were a few hard landings but better than the alternative. I can imagine one thinking as it left the nest 'what the HELL have I done?' That's kind of where we were at times, fly or take whatever comes. Jumping out into the unknown is the first step.

As the settling in continued at times I would walk the streets and trails in part just out of boredom. One afternoon I was just milling along and suddenly there it was...a roughed up discarded porn magazine just lying on the side of the road. I could have been in the right place at the right time or the exact opposite. I picked it up and began to turn pages and I believe my eyes got as big as dinner plates, accompanied by butterflies. WOW!

These girls were umm, touching themselves in places and ways my little brain didn't comprehend, and seemingly looking right at me. I was for the first time seeing parts of girls I had never given thought to before and I was astonished, mesmerized. I knew they had those fun bags under their shirts but the actual knowing kind of took a bit of excitement away, leaving only a kids fantasy. So, my love of music now had a rival, a strong unrelenting rival. I had to see and learn more, much much more.

At this point I had never had the old birds and bees talk, I suppose it wasn't Scott's place to do so, no hard feelings there. I recall hearing I would have that talk one day and I kinda knew the subject matter but could make no sense of it. Birds and bees do the nasty together? Is that where hummingbirds came from? What do birds and bees have to do with a kid's morning wood? Wood, cork, whatever. Is that how a woodpecker got it's name? Seems to me something more appropriate might have been the old beaver and rooster talk.

I do remember hearing sex once, while staying at a friend's house. This girl was just hollering and moaning so loud I thought "well that doesn't sound pleasurable at all!!" Did she step in a bear trap? Unfortunately I was only taught in Sunday school that such things were sinful and disgraceful. I believe the subject was addressed as the 'original sin' whereby man gave into temptation. A sinful act that one should ask forgiveness for. Well, if you do it right then you may feel the need to ask forgiveness! On the other hand if it wasn't right, just ask the one next to you for forgiveness. If it wasn't sinful at the start maybe you're just not applying yourself. A lot of those preaching that belief have 6 or 7 kids which begs the question...did either find an ounce of enjoyment while attempting pregnancy? It's like going to a movie theatre, sleeping throughout the entire film and claiming later it just wasn't that good.

The same Sunday school "teacher" when speaking on matters of the flesh would quickly get rather animated which immediately turned to frustration. Thinking back he didn't know what the hell he was talking about, how to verbalize anything and it just made him so uncomfortable.

In his mind he knew preaching the sins of the flesh to kids contradicted the exact thing he had done himself two nights before. The fact that it was over for him in 3 minutes isn't the point, his words were contradictory, hypocritical. Oh, and don't be talking about it or looking at pictures or whatever. "Sex should be between you and the person you're doing it to!!" someone said. OK sir, I see your personal view on the matter but, you might want to rephrase that!

Years later with hindsight in mind, I can easily picture the poor old guy walking out of the little church classroom wiping the nervous sweat off of his forehead, face red as a baboons' ass. The very message he just tried uncomfortably to deliver probably had him to the point he'd stick his penis in a bush if he thought a horny snake was in there. I'd be willing to bet he drove home to the wife with speeds of up to 40 mph...I'm not judging anything other than his ill prepared life's lesson for others and his hypocritical teachings of what not to do. Unless of course you can drive like a bat out of hell in order to do those same things before the wife goes to bed. I'm sure that's why he kept looking at his watch, it must have been 3:30 pm or so, bedtime being at 5:00, you get the idea.

I just really wish someone had said "look, sex is a natural thing, not a one way ticket to eternal suffering." I would learn about girls and their wonders as I had the drums, self-taught mixed with a little embarrassment and a few blisters. The two subjects were clearly not related but demanded investigation. On one hand you had the loud noise, lights, sweating, applause and encores. Come to think of it maybe they are related.

When I first heard someone mention foreplay I thought it meant four people. When I learned the actual meaning I knew I had far to go. When asked which came first, the chicken or the egg, from what I'd heard in passing I'd say the one smoking the cigarette. As a rookie starter there was no foreplay, I had maybe 2 plays. I really endeavored to learn as much as possible, which entails much practice.

Referring back to that life changing smut magazine it only served to push my curiosity over the edge. I knew my little trouser mouse had another function and for a time it resembled a pistol grip. I suppose it was meant to be, no one was going to educate me or had attempted to so it fell back on Miss Never say No-vember, my new friend. There may have been an ad or two about beer or watches, probably.

In the interim sis and I were established and running around with friends like Roach, Mutt, Buzz and of course guys were around also. Someone once said a person blooms where they are planted but I don't think they were speaking of poison ivy. If contracted, you usually can't be specific where it came from and once you realize you've been exposed it's every damn where. There are times when a person just has to ride it out and keep their hands away from certain things, dammit.

Alcohol was always in the picture and would remain so. An invention from long ago, a product that provides courage, astounding decision making, alienation and pain, all in a handy liquid form. In all of my years I can say that I only blacked out once, from 1987 to about 2001. Not surprising considering I had my first fake ID at barely 16, and it never failed once. When we celebrated my 18th my favorite server was quite shocked as she had been serving me for some time.

Marijuana was the dominate choice wherever we roamed, readily available and cheap. In those days one could purchase a sandwich bag, full and thick for about $40 give or take. That amount however was harder to come by at the time as $40 wasn't always available. Unavoidably came the hash and as much as I hate to say, LSD. I am truly not happy or proud of that choice but I did partake about 15 times or so. It was such a bizarre high for me, but I wasn't me, and I wasn't here or there, just out there. I thank the good Lord for deliverance from that self-inflicted nightmare.

My big sis was blazing a trail of sorts in the community on her own, one that I would follow to a degree. Sis was truly a good person who seemingly was just a magnet for trouble in one form or another. The big difference between the 2 of us was that she always got caught doing something whereas I didn't. She brought that up several times with me. Looking back she was right, she had either left a clue of sorts or some evidence pointing to her. While she was being interrogated and punished I was in the background incognito doing the same things or worse.

I suppose I didn't contribute a lot to her benefit back then by getting on her nerves constantly. It really pissed her off when I invaded her privacy, especially her being a young lady. I suppose I was a bit of a terror.

There were bullies in our neighborhood that hounded and harassed her on a daily basis, female bullies that honestly were intimidating. She fought occasionally, no more than 10 times a week but only out of necessity. In that period, location and time, to not fight would have been twice as bad. It did bother me much to see her get physical with girls who cared little about their appearance in the first place, and the only concern about their reputation was how bad it could get. They didn't care if they got a black eye or bloody lip and sis made sure they did. Typically those types of things were just traded back and forth.

In a very short stretch she had been a truant from school, runaway from home, been sent to a "special" residence and by 13 or so left to stay with relatives far away, resulting in the 2 of us not seeing each other for years.

I really wasn't affected at that time because of all the hardness we had experienced thus far but hidden within me was the loss of my sister which I somehow just buried, guess I learned how to do that way too early. I smile now because she's my sis and I laugh because there's nothing she can do about it. She had truly gone away, created a new life and style, beat all odds, eventually becoming a mom herself and solidly determined she would only return for brief visits. She loved her new self and created her own place in life too far away. Prior to her leaving she had laid the foundation of what to accept, what to refuse to accept and was leaving me to build upon it so to speak. I did inherit just a bit of her reputation by association, which would prove to be unnecessary really, my own would trump hers. I love her much and we see and talk to each other as often as possible. Who knows how life would have turned out had she not relocated?

At school I became very popular quickly for all the wrong reasons. I was always in trouble for stupid shit like little fights or mouthing off, maybe setting off a firecracker or two. Smoking in the bathroom was something done in-between every class and at times the bathroom looked like a sauna. Typically there was more than just tobacco smoke. I do recall a vice principal bursting in once, a rarity. He walked through pointing to everyone he'd actually seen smoking and invited them to the office. When he got to the end of the line and turned around he got so mad, furious. All the ones he had passed first and ordered to the office were finishing their smokes before they left, knowing they were already in trouble anyway. We couldn't help but laugh at his red faced disbelief.

I became a regular fixture in the principal's office for various reasons to the degree that the yearbook committee just took my picture there, and in the book it went. I still have that yearbook today. I got even though, breaking into the school one sunny Saturday and riding my skateboard down the hallways while eating lunchroom ice cream at their expense. No breaking, just entering through a window that was slightly ajar which really was a sirens song to a young punk kid searching for just such a thing. I did have a partner in crime that day which allows the sense of boldness or being untouchable. In reality we were so ignorant to what might have been, the same as if he had said to me "I dare you to walk over to that rattlesnake and try to pet it". All things considered I'm glad I never heard that dare.

Over a short amount of time we became proficient at shoplifting, acquiring certain things, finding trouble at any turn, or creating it, running the roads, just not giving a shit. The partying and drinking had become a lifestyle and we did what we wanted no matter the cost. It's highly likely we retired a Mexican drug lord in short time. Stranger still, we played sports as normal kids did at other schools with one big exception, we couldn't wait to smoke a bowl and have a beer at the end of practice. Believe me many dads were missing beers, usually didn't realize it though. One year we actually went undefeated and won the district championship, kind of bizarre in that we smoked, toked, drank and nursed many hangovers in the 90 degree heat of practice. The cheerleading squad would practice close by and at times in-between plays I'd hear the cheer "Gimme an N, Gimme an E," then silence. Out of curiosity I'd glance over quickly to see a little cat fight happening, scratching, name calling and rolling on the ground. Knowing most of them to some degree, they were likely hungover also. After a few minutes they'd get up, scratched all over and looking like they just got off of some tequila fueled hay ride and try to act normal. Even funnier, I do remember our coaches commenting at times about how hard we hit and gang tackled, raising hell because occasionally it was someone on the sidelines, not even in the game.

I cannot fathom how but due to our undefeated championship season we had earned a trip to New York. Of course we were excited beyond reason, we had only seen pictures and heard things prior. Corners had been cut of course considering the cost and number of players. I believe some of my teammates traveled with their court appointed chaperones to conserve gas and also ease some minds.

I was amazed at the lights, the sheer size of the place, the buildings were so unbelievable. Hell the tallest structure we'd seen in our vicinity was maybe 3 stories and basically used to smoke weed in, some call them deer stands. The narrow streets, teeny restaurants, and a never ending sea of people who said anything, everything on their mind at the time. I couldn't help but wonder if car horns were new to them because used them incessantly for no apparent reason. Then came the adult shit again.

I went into a narrow little shop just to get candy or something and was looking at the options. Suddenly and without any cause this guy comes into the little aisle I was in hollering "YOU, OUT OF MY STORE NOW"! spoken in some accent I'd never heard. His demeanor and abrupt nature, combined with the presence of what appeared to be a giant cloth ice cream cone on his head startled me and I got out quickly. Of course later I would learn that people there hadn't seen that many caucasions grouped together other than passing by a hockey rink, it frightened them. In any event I truly hadn't done anything!

I did mention corners had been cut whereby two to three of us together were staying with the families of our opponents we would eventually meet on the gridiron. That being the case we were very much in the heart of outer NYC, neighborhoods with very slender but tall homes. It might as well have been another planet from our point of view. Absolutely everything was different, houses, streets, accents, subways, taxis, screaming and cursing dusk to dawn, traffic, hookers, food, every damn thing. Had they come to our homes it would likely have been even more odd. One thing that stood out immediately was the lack of space between the houses. In some cases there couldn't have been more than 8 feet in between two of them. The kids, our rivals, had been given some freedom I assume to give us a showing of their neighborhoods and surroundings. That's when the real differences were made clear, really something to experience.

Women holding a screen door open yelling, cussing and screaming about kids in the street. Voices from any given direction saying things like "Antonee, gat ovah here now," or "das what I said, das what I said," or perhaps "get a lodge pie, yeh a lodge pie over dare from Vinny on twelf n turd." Very memorable, I would prefer that incident with the sheik wasn't just as memorable. Good bye to the big apple and once again back to apple sauce.

Football season over means too much free time for idle hands so inevitably we wander, and wonder. Spurts of delinquency becoming more frequent. As for minor thefts, horrible as it was, we never took anything of value but I think just wanted the rush. There may have been an occasional brick through a window of uninhabited places so nothing really was taken. We hitchhiked to places with people we did not know traveling hundreds of miles in driving sleet and snow, eating raw eggs right out of the package for reasons unknown. We didn't require reasons or even plans sometimes. Our only question was "why not"?

There was an abandoned lot not too far from the neighborhood that once was a very small amusement park. By now the rides were gone leaving only a few small buildings. We would go there on occasion to smoke, hang out, ride bikes. One day however curiosity had gotten the best of us, we simply had to know what was in those buildings. Of course we didn't have keys, much less permission but when did that ever matter? We broke windows and doors and got in, rummaged through drawers and shelves, nothing of much interest there but we took a few tokens. Due to our rough entrance we had some cuts on arms and hands, stepped on large nails, maybe a couple of other small punctures. When we would go home bleeding, scraped up or limping it was always the best idea to have a story straight and stick to it, that's the moral of that incident. Also, be prepared to explain where you "*found*" 10,000 straws.

One incident stands out on it's own though. We did steal a vehicle, right out of the driveway in the dead of night. The key had been left in the ignition and well, that was not wise. We drove around a bit, acting like idiots, almost flipped it over unconcerned about icy, wet conditions. We managed to return it as it was, minus some gas and tread. I have no recollection of exactly where we were or how we got to the next stop or even home. I don't know if the owners ever knew. That night does bother me when I consider the actual vehicle theft, danger to others on the road, destroying that vehicle and possibly ourselves.

School was unpleasant, unwanted and boring. I didn't learn or test well and simply didn't care for it. For some time there was no air conditioning, no amenities whatsoever. Anywhere you looked showed the age of the building in spite of fresh paint occasionally. Our favorite area was of course the outside smoking pit. Yes indeed in those days it was allowed and it stayed packed. Soon I would have other things to concentrate on in the nice form of Miss Baker.

Young, nice, very engaging and hot as hell. Now a lot of us had a crush on a teacher or whatever, but she would prove to be different and quite surprising to say the very least. Thank you smut magazine!

We would talk after class at times, just bullshit and joke around. Before long she would occasionally give me a ride home and let her hair down a little, letting the cuss words fly. Things progressed at light speed from there. All of a sudden we were camping by a creek, running the roads, drinking, smoking pot. We actually traveled across 2 or 3 state lines at one point and stayed in a hotel which was not a hurtful or uncomfortable time, very memorable. The talk was that I was taken advantage of or coerced or manipulated, in private they probably thought what a lucky little bastard. Rumors had been circulating and one particular day a classmate approached me with a picture that had been ripped out of some magazine like the one I had found. There she was, miss teacher, posing in ways that some naked gymnast could only do. I did take it to her so that it wouldn't circulate or end up in the wrong hands. She looked at it quickly, threw her head back and took a deep breath, then crumbled it in her hand and walked quickly away. She wasn't around long afterwards.

After some time had passed I heard she was now at another school in another town some miles away. The number of miles and lack of transportation were of no matter. Somehow 3 or 4 of us idiots got together and managed to secure a ride in order to pay a surprise visit. One must keep in mind things were much different then in terms of security and such. We made our way to that school and marched right through a side door as if we were students. It must have been painfully clear we were not. Strolling through the packed cafeteria and down hallways until we found her classroom and proceeded to walk right in as she was teaching. The look on her face at first was shock, then a little grin, finally the look of panic considering she might have to explain this bizarre behavior. We just spoke very quickly and exited before trouble came, which I'm sure it did. That was the end of that. Looking back I can't determine if I was her experiment or vice versa. After some years had passed and thoughts processed I realized there was more than one lesson involved in that charade, one of which I hadn't taken in.

She and I were clearly far apart considering age, giving her experience, control over emotion as well as control over times spent together. In short she had zero emotional attachment or feelings whereas I had fallen into the painful, unforgiving place of caring and obsession to some degree. I thought maybe I was special or something for a spell. That particular lesson and the grief that followed greets everyone at some stage in life, probably not in that manner though. If I were a lab rat so to speak, at least I got some cheese, and from a good source.

While all the insanity was taking place I still kept up with my music and learning, had been in my first band and continued my quest for knowledge of the girls. I had been somewhat educated as to what to do and how but there was much to learn I theorized and I was committed. Two girls in particular elevated me to a previously unknown level.

One of my heathen friends had a girlfriend that didn't belong. That is to say she was so sweet and innocent to our reality, definitely a heartbreaker. When she smiled or laughed her eyes almost shut and her cheeks lit up. She was maybe a year older than me, absolutely gorgeous and she knew my thoughts. Long story short, one night at a party my friend passed out and I became a shark smelling blood in the water. My thoughts were not honorable for either of them, my buddy after all was my partner. I guess I convinced myself that other horny young men were going to attempt something with her sooner rather than later and decided to be her knight in denim armor.

About 5 minutes after he took a bourbon nap the electricity between us was immediate, we could sense what was coming in our bones. In fact a few others had even sensed something between the two of us without each being even in the same room. We mingled and chatted a bit and finally interfaced, both of us grinning and excited as two could be. Within a few short minutes we stepped outside, quickly found privacy in the form of a comfortable back seat and honestly, for some time that was the only reality on the planet. I believe a sasquatch with a marching band drum kit could have tap danced on the hood while juggling two chainsaws and neither of us would have had a clue.

As we began to get better acquainted she said something that really got my attention, and changed me a bit. Four beautiful, simple words I've never forgotten, "be easy with me..." Damn damn damn. What she was saying was "I'm in your care, I'm trusting you, do whatever you want, but be easy..." I just about melted. I liken those words to spraying a bear in the face with mace made from fresh honey. Here I am, a young half man with only so much experience, trying to um, keep it together and you're gonna say some shit like that to me?? To this day those four words remain probably the sexiest thing any girl ever said to me.

I was easy with her as she delicately requested, and indeed I did whatever I wanted, soft and gentle as I could be over every inch of her. The only impressions I got from her were 'keep going' and 'oh damn!'. We had a very special well known song that was ours and without specificity the lyrics eluded to how we came together for one special highly anticipated night, knowing it was coming, and just got it over with so to speak. We would talk about that night years later, several times. Hell even now it makes me want to smoke just thinking about it.

On the opposite end, the cheerleader. Beautiful, extremely fit, tons of self-confidence. The exercise and workouts were clearly evident, she could've probably cracked walnuts with her ass cheeks. I'm not sure if she had been to some kind of sex farm or seminar but for her age she was very well informed and experienced. On one special evening, she said she wanted to show me something and she did.

She laid out on her bed and began rubbing herself very slowly, working her way to her impressive breasts and south from there. She simply said "I want you to watch" and began removing anything not made of skin. If that wasn't enough, she reached under a pillow and pulled out her inanimate friend and I was amazed at what she did with it, repeatedly and in multiple places. No hesitation, no inhibition, just watching me watch her with this look of complete satisfaction. I have to say I was hypnotized briefly and it was burnt into my memory. Eventually she had worn herself out and said "I'll see you tomorrow", pulled the covers up and I left, pants on fire. Unbelievable, unforgettable, un everything else. I truly believe most of the adrenaline was due to the fact that her parents were right across the hall. That alone got me thinking, she did get her looks from her mom, is mom possibly that outgoing also? I hadn't heard anyone say MILF in those days but it would've been applicable.

Prior to my deep indulgence into the girls I learned a little something unintended and very much unwanted. I suppose I was in my very early teens and was walking into some very large outdoor flea market-yard sale event. It was a nice set up with overhead cover, tables, food etc... Before I actually got to the official entrance a car pulled up beside me and stopped, some guy hanging his head out of the window with a suspicious looking grin. He said "hey, how you doin' buddy, you need a ride"? It was clear I did not need a ride, nor make any effort to get one. As the day passed, along with subsequent days I realized he was a stalker, an evil man wanting me to get close enough so as to grab me or whatever. Recalling that evil clown look he had there was no doubt, and the ridiculous offer of a ride when I'm clearly approaching my destination. I felt so uneasy after the fact, he was definitely 3 times my size, and I thought of stories about so many missing young people. If only I had been a few years older I might have walked over to his window smiling, hate and anger building with each step. I wouldn't have needed any more than maybe 3 or 4 actual steps honestly before unleashing. Asshole came looking for a victim, left looking for a doctor, and I would just claim self-defense. Thinking back now self-defense might have been hard to sell as the plaintiff was still in the vehicle and buckled as well.

Being a pedophile is unforgiveable as is, but a homosexual kidnapping pedophile? I suppose that's the reckoning for approaching very young, unsuspecting people and likewise the need for an ambush. In my circumstance he was just too damn excited, too eager, that evil look behind the smile was unmistakable. I'm no judge or jury but given the chance, I would make sure he never saw a judge or jury. I've never spoken of that incident prior to now.

Summing up, my early years were at times chaotic and confusing. I had all the love at home that one needed and then some. The older I got however, the less I was at home. Things certainly got out of hand and at times going a bit further. Occasionally I would hear people say "oh I've heard about you" and brush it off as a joke. I thought to myself whatever you heard isn't true, it's worse. I've heard about you likewise, having to replace broken windows and doors all over the place...asshole.

We survived and we had one more move to make, a new town not too far away but worlds apart. I was excited, more than ready to leave my existence and not having a clue how things would change. I knew what I knew from my old neighborhood and it took very little time to recognize things would be much, much different. In that little life span I had learned fear, hate, infatuation, disdain, physical pain and distrust. I don't admit this with any pride at all but very slowly I realized the value in keeping certain things from the adults, most notably mom. I couldn't stand to be the source of her disappointment or heartache, she was already distraught over my sis. Being evasive and ambiguous is great in life if you're a spy or hired assassin. My point being I only kept polishing that skill, thus much of my life and being where make believe. It can't be undone, neither can a ton of guilt. Guilt is a cancer, a killer, don't attempt to live that way.

I had been introduced to the adult drug world and likewise the adult world of carnal knowledge. Not that entire world, just a couple vacation spots. What I came away with in that time was simple to me, adults are untrustworthy, adults have authority so authority is bad also. Chemical use is permissible, alcohol as well, fighting is sometimes inevitable and girls are wonderous and amazing. Yes they cry at times for no apparent reason and talk a lot but that's easily overlooked. That was the mindset of my young punk ass, playing with the cards I was dealt. My little world was taking shape, unknown to me at that time. I can say now things really just happened too quickly and would have been better suited for someone at an older age, that can't be denied. I am comfortable in saying that parents or grandparents, even if just a little on the party side would agree. My mom did no wrong, in fact went beyond the call of duty. In her *defense I'll say this, what you don't know you don't know. I did everything in my power to keep her from knowing things that would cause concern or hurt. That was perpetrated by me and I swallowed all that shit for so long. Looking back, mom knew much more than I believed.*

STAGE 2

The newer vicinity was far apart from the old, visually the whole atmosphere was amazing, houses and yards were nice and clean, the roads were maintained, mailboxes didn't have deer antlers or beer stickers. There was an unmistakable absence of cars on cinderblocks and just as noticeably the women here knew of bras. I was accustomed to seeing them in a floor or floorboard, occasionally where they belonged, a door knob. These girls used them on a regular basis and it occurred to me these bras are not just going to magically fall off as before, genuine effort would have to be applied which at first horrified me. I would have to apply myself somehow, someway. The thing is I didn't really care for me so why apply anything. I very much needed to, and wanted to be someone else. Not the easiest thing to take on, but there wasn't another option really. My saving grace was the fact that I was new, unknown and the past was just that. I shed my old self the same as any other snake.

My new school was more than new to me but had only been built a few years earlier so new all around. As I walked and began to get acquainted there it was almost as if it were some futuristic show. A very up to date appearance, several levels, carpeting, air conditioning, amazing.

I was clearly now in a much different world and I knew I had to adapt which I was willing and excited to do. I began to dress much differently and develop a better persona. Most importantly how I presented myself to others, including my speech. I learned of such things as collared shirts and men without baseball caps. Sweet fancy Moses enough with the damn baseball caps. I was transforming like a chameleon and letting go of my short past. One of my best achievements was actual learning, studying in my new beautiful school, willingly. I thirsted for education I never had appreciated and very quickly became an honor student with top notch grades that I maintained throughout. It's astounding what can be accomplished with minimal effort.

There is simply no question or comparison, having knowledge and understanding is, you know, better than that other thing. Honestly I never studied very long or hard even prior to tests or exams. I just soaked everything in right from the classroom by listening. If a subject was difficult to follow or not quite clear I just associated the matter with a color or shape, mostly with a word that would rhyme with the subject at hand, or perhaps I had been noticing the girl 2 rows over and would then do the same. For example, if I needed to remember the date 1744 for whatever reason I might think...'she's probably not quite 17, but those legs have got to be 44 inches long'....perhaps the subject was a planet or our solar system...I might put the planet Uranus in my mind and connect her to that word in some kind of way, something as simple as Uranus, Heranus, whatever works. In all seriousness learning by association was miraculous for me personally, my success with testing is the proof. The downside, when the teacher asked me to come up and point out Uranus for the class I just couldn't. If I had stood up I probably could have pointed to it without a finger, but I knew where Uranus was! I could test well, have a little grin and be horny all at the same time, cigarette waiting.

Things that I thought silly before were now thought provoking and leading, causing me to really contemplate and want more. I do admit I also had one or two art classes, the easiest of the bunch, but they were taken seriously as well as some of my work would be prominently displayed for all to see. My art, my creations in a large display case within the main entrance. It made me a little proud and that feeling was also somewhat new to me.

There were some that knew or could tell I was a bit of an outsider and I expected that. After all a pig wearing a pearl necklace remains a pig. One particular day as I was walking to the school entrance a bus began pulling up with students preparing to start their day. Three young men were hanging their heads out of the windows just carrying on and loving life when one of them made a derogatory statement directed at me which I didn't care for.

I continued on and knowing where the bus would stop I waited with a hint of nervous energy and proceeded to put my game face on. When the trio began to leave that comfort zone they were a little surprised. The first one said "I didn't say anything dude," followed by number two who claimed they thought I was someone else and began apologizing. Well, I was someone else dammit and I had made it known right then and there to kind of let me be. I don't recall any further issues from that point. From there I just minded my business and continued to study and learn, never stopped toking and saw no effects, my grades were in the top of the class consistently. Change that I had been needing had come finally, but I had no idea just how much and how quickly change can change.

In short time I was befriended by someone that would become as close to a brother as possible, Drew. He had grown up in a single parent home along with an older brother Barry and an even older sister Sam. The father who was disabled slightly and always home was a great guy. I was welcomed in without question and became a regular fixture there, coming and going as I pleased with full access to the house any day or time without knocking whether someone was home or not. I would have access to any food, automobiles and for some time basically lived there. I had yet another education coming.

Barry not only had been around but was still getting around so the drugs were flowing freely and cocaine was now making a big debut. He wasn't always the most agreeable person in the world but he showed me a few things in his world. Sister Sam, 7 or 8 years older than me and somewhat immodest would also show me some things, but that was yet to come.

The amount of craziness and substance abuse is immeasurable. The parties and stories thereof would become almost legendary, the rest of the neighborhood was not happy. There are two circumstances that made a bit of a mark on me concerning my new adoptive family, two out of 1000 or more, the first not real pleasant.

We had all taken an excursion to the beach and others would be there as well. Coolers packed, bowls packed, the weather was perfect and at some point I decided to hit the waves unaccompanied.

I had gone out not too far as I recall, maybe 60 yards and I was getting a little winded so I started on back to shore. I swam for a bit and noticed I was getting more tired, the waves had begun to come over my head some and I realized not only was I not making progress but was further out. I swam harder, the waves got a little bigger and by now I was running out of steam quickly. Something was very wrong and I yelled out for help but I know now that was useless due to the ambient every day beach sounds.

Now I'm ingesting more water, trying to spit it out which has depleted my oxygen to a minimum, I'm a little further out and my arms feel like stones. Panic turned my swimming into flailing and eventually I started going under over and over. I vividly recall knowing the next time will be the last because I could do no more and it happened immediately. Everything was now silent, I felt no dread and I wasn't panicking but more or less along for the ride. I do remember a sad sense very quickly realizing that I was going to die but as others have said in that situation, drowning seems the most peaceful way to let go assuming you're not having a leg chewed off while it happens. Honestly there was some peace in that moment as I just accepted the outcome. Suddenly a hand and then an arm followed by fresh air and a surfboard. Someone had seen my struggles and reacted, taking my arms and draping them across the board where I collapsed and watched as he did the same. We were now both in the grip of the riptide but this guy knew, don't fight it just hang on and we'll make it to shore which we did albeit about a third of a mile from where I should be. We crawled our way up onto the beach and it was over.

My closest encounter with near sudden death and the "close call" scenario was entirely too close. Additionally, no one who had remained on the beach showed concern or interest or caring of any kind. That's the kind of thing that lets a person know where they stand, or perhaps where the body is found.

This event remained strong for several reasons, the first of which being as with the dog attack I was alone. Secondly it happened so quickly with no warning and I realized later I was so very close to just disappearing. Lastly I did learn without a doubt that I was susceptible to being taken out of existence at any time, thus I was mortal. Damn, I don't think I'd ever considered that.

The second event is much more warming to reflect on as I have at times thanks to Drew's sis Sam. How to describe her is simple, a guy's girl. Fun as hell, didn't give a shit and never did. To me she was the picture of the girl next door as they say, if you happen to live next door to a somewhat older sailor mouthed nymphomaniac. The large difference between our ages was definitely intimidating at that time but not so much as to shy away. That being said, when people speak of having butterflies in their stomach, I had more of an ostrich. I'm sure there must have been times when swimming trunks or the like would have given my thoughts away.

She was a guy's girl, cute as hell, funny, very straightforward. A mix of blonde reddish hair, body built for sin and a mouth to go with it. She was one to not be taken lightly, in fact a small first aid kit might have been appropriate. In either case the curiosity and drive couldn't be overcome. To set the stage we had been around each other long enough by this time that we had been sending little signs to each other by virtue of inside jokes or passing eye contact. The quick eye contact was immediately followed by a smirk from both. I always had imagined things but dismissed those thoughts because of the circumstances and age difference. I knew her family as my own, her dad and brothers could never know my thoughts much less anything to follow. I contemplated on that dilemma seemingly forever, in reality about 25 minutes. Sam was different however, for her it took 15 minutes. We definitely had similar thoughts and ideas, but staying ahead of the game she had plans.

One night after much alcohol things began to wind down as the hours went by and people were either passing out or had left. Sam was sitting next to me and said " we need to get you to bed before you fall out." Sweet Sam, thinking only of my best interests, not. I was escorted to a bedroom and took off my visual clothing and got horizontal, she left to do whatever.

I was awakened sometime afterward to her disrobing slowly and quietly, there were still others in the vicinity after all. She crept into bed and very gently cozied up to me resting her head on my shoulder and her hand on my chest, and then the fingernails very lightly teasing. I was still quite inebriated but I damn sure knew who it was and kind of what was taking place, I just couldn't move. She began rubbing my chest, then my stomach and in an instant her hand was under the elastic that held me in. Soft and slow gripping and grabbing with much patience, then some pressure and backing off again. Again I was not totally in control of myself but I wasn't dead either.

There are no words to say how quickly she moved when her hand was done. I swear before I could blink she raised up and jerked the covers off completely and the underwear as well, into the floor and I laid there like a turtle without a shell. She put her head down on my chest and began kissing, moving on to my stomach and then Christmas. There had been no words, eye contact or any other pointless waste of time. There was apparently a job to do and it had to be done.

If one chose to get technical, I was pretty much raped. Blissfully, enthusiastically and with my full cooperation, that being I put up zero resistance. Having said that, for the love of GOD please don't read anything into that such as making fun of an actual sexual assault or the real brutality of rape. It's deplorable, unforgiveable and heinous. I strive only to express my individual thoughts and feelings as they were at certain ages and times. I was not assaulted, it's hard to assault the willing.

In terms of sexual knowledge I was a freshman whereas Sam had graduated with honors and apparently was seeking a degree or the role of assistant professor. That special night she did not relent one bit but instead had an attitude of cockiness as in "look what I can do!" In the end things did indeed end well for both. She knew what she and I both had been wanting and we both got it. Hell I think at one point she screamed out her own name.

In the morning when I stumbled into the kitchen she was there along with a few others nursing themselves. We glanced at each other and her expression was one of a devilish smirk of satisfaction, nasty damn hot ass thing. As hungover as I was 15 minutes prior, the little smartass smirk on her face took that all away. I learned in the coming weeks that what happened was just a rehearsal, she would go on to show me more and more, sometimes in a vehicle, sometimes sneaking away from others during a party or celebration, one reenactment of the first encounter. I likewise was perfectly at ease grabbing, touching, pulling, ordering or firmly requesting if preferred, or just watching. That eye to eye thing in the midst of a major throwdown is incredible. Throw in some dirty talk and it's like "waiter, check please!!! NOW!" The downside, I had pretty much committed an unforgiveable act, participating in immoral behavior with the only daughter/sister of a family that made me just as much a part of the family as any other. In the very beginning she was like my sister but feelings, people change. No doubt they would have been mortified, so that bothers me.

Returning to a more traditional education, while heading to a class one day I was just taking everything in and then there she was. Sitting in her classroom waiting for the bell to ring was this young stunning girl, front row of the class. I remember thinking there were many available seats in the rear, she's a goody girl. I walked by that room the next few days always looking and she knew for sure, glancing at me and quickly putting her head down. One day she stood outside the room engaged with no one, she had waited for me to come by purposely. I said hi, she said hi and smiled, we talked for maybe one minute before the bell rang and decided to meet after class. What was said in those minutes was irrelevant, she could have said something about a stick or bread, it didn't matter. I did have her name now, Melissa. Another life changing event was on the horizon in more than one way.

What makes someone desirable is a question best answered on an individual basis. For me it could be several things such as a smile, a beautiful face or the eyes or personality, of course the physical attributes. Certainly there were occasions where just a pulse was enough that thought goes for men and women both, though 98% wouldn't admit. It's like the porn industry, nobody ever admits partaking yet as a whole the industry is worth about a billion, seriously. I rented a few movies in my past but that still leaves somewhere in the vicinity of a billion. I couldn't be the only one.

Back to the jaw dropping insanely hot Melissa. After giving her rides home from school a few times I finally asked her out to which she happily said yes. I met the parents who were very nice and welcoming, and before our first outing her dad said "I'd like to have her back by 9:00" and I thought to myself 9:00 next Tuesday, no problem sir. In reality I could have spent that much time with her just watching her sleep, water and food unnecessary. Our first couple of outings were nothing impressive but just getting better acquainted, our kissing was getting more intense and lengthy but I kept my hands and self in control.

About the fourth date I decided we would go to a place not well traveled where the view was amazing, overlooking miles of lights and any other potential visitors were only there for the same. In the car we were always joined at the hip so to speak and this night was no different. All of the windows were down and the perfect breeze was blowing as we started mouthing and kissing with a bit more intensity than what we had done before. Moving like a sloth I began moving my hands around her shoulders and back while her arms were wrapped tight around my neck, where they remained. I touched her with the same degree of care one might use while trying to split an atom under a microscope. I sensed no hesitation at all from her, maybe a tiny bit of nervousness but I clearly had the impression to move forward, just respectfully slowly. Until I had some implication to stop there would be none, the situation was equivalent to her being steel and myself a magnet. One of those giant magnets seen in a junkyard, ain't letting go.

As a visual the vehicle was very large with upholstered bench seats front and back with the only difference being that pesky steering wheel. After much kissing and rubbing we decided to get in the back seat and again it was large and comfortable. Picking up where we left off was immediate and there was no stopping now. The first button on her shirt was taken out of commission followed by heavier breathing, then the next and so on. It was a slow deliberate process, probably fifteen minutes for no more than five buttons, with no objections and finally no buttons were left. I'll always remember when my hand touched her stomach and the small of her back how her skin was so so soft and delicate in a way. When I finally put my hand on her bra the sensation seemed new to her but not unwelcome. When I pushed that bra up and out of the way it was if I'd never done it before and she'd not had it done before. Every sense was heightened and I thought how fortunate it was those crickets make almost the same sound as a zipper being operated, so I went with that strange thought and chimed in with them, the zippers being the last obstacle.

I know of no other way to describe the next hour or so other than she was just mine, like a buffet as in the more you see the more you want. That old saying 'my eyes were bigger than my stomach' did not apply in this case, not remotely. I did what I could to ensure she felt secure and comfortable. I'm sure I left a gentle mark or two on her that only she could see later, and I'm pretty sure I visited places that she didn't know she had. I say that because every inch of her was visited at least twice and had time magically stopped the count would be easily double digits. She was relatively quiet throughout, which was so damn sexy but her hip movements and the strong grip on my back were very telling. In short time she just let go, I'll never forget how I physically felt her thighs trembling and her hands searching for something to grasp, which turned out to be any damn thing within reach including her own self. When time came to take her home I did not want to, not even a little. She felt the same. She made my damn teeth sweat.

For the first time in a relationship I had to consider pregnancy unintentional or not. As I thought about protection and what to do it became clear I was really uninformed. Looking over the condom selection just left more questions. First there were the three sizes, small, medium and leg. I wasn't going to buy the small, and the leg size might have made me look like a clown with those giant shoes on. This ribbed for her pleasure thing seemed a bit unfair to me, could I not turn it inside out for my pleasure? In the end I got nothing and to this very day have never had one on. I suppose I'm fortunate to have not contracted anything or had some ailment named after me.

Our relationship grew more intense with each outing, the ease of my exploring her physically was gifted to me by her and the heat wasn't lessening. I can say that she was touched and kissed as softly as I could top to bottom and whatever was in between those parameters, despite my wanting to just eat her alive.

Very sadly things changed much too quickly and for no honorable or decent reason, that being my dumb ass. I'd never had those feelings before and I was becoming conflicted and unsure. Her feelings for me were so incredibly strong and growing as were mine and I began to feel that pressure as in suffocation. In less than a year of meeting I simply walked away, not a disappearing act but just called it quits. It did indeed hurt her I know and I did regret that decision greatly. When a little time had passed I knew full well I screwed up, I still had those feelings and I tried to find her over and over but it wasn't to be. What a dumb shit thing I had done, I knew any young man within 400 miles would step over their own mother just to take her on a date, yes she was like that. I really fucked that up.

It has often been said that things happen for a reason, I agree to some extent. I would think it highly unlikely that I would have met my wife further down the road had I not turned from her, and I would take nothing at all for our marriage and time together. Likewise Melissa would not have married and had kids with the one it was meant to be for her and that's great, apparently predestined. If I could, even through this writing, I just always wanted to say I'm so damn sorry for the way I left, how I left, I know it hurt and I can offer no reasoning, I'm just sorry.

So there were two lessons I learned that stuck with me. I did have the capability for intense love for someone that had been dormant until then, I also realized that I had done the same thing my father had done and just walked away never to see her again. Into the soul box.

Navigating through a first love and the insanities of my second family were kind of equalized by my first job, which would come to be the biggest life changing event to date and likely evermore. Unbeknownst to me it would bring so many changes in countless ways that literally recreated me inside and out, physically, emotionally and mentally. I was about to die and be reborn.

A friend of a friend had gotten me a job with a relatively small business that specialized in custom made shirts and such, having whatever logo or wording a customer required. Of the 30 or so employees most were artists and creative in their own rights, others were office and payroll types, but one commonality was they were just crazy fun loving people in this environment that had few boundaries.

The biggest factor by far with this job was the clear age difference. Not only was I the newest hire, but definitely the baby of the bunch. I was in high school of course, the youngest ones there had graduated some five years before, not sure how. That factor was never a concern in any way because at the time it was a non-issue. Over a very short amount of time it would be the building foundation of who I really am today, no exaggeration. The day I started working there was key to all that followed. My future brothers and sisters, my personal internal and external recreation, the very welcome bonfire of my former self, lifestyle, image, most certainly my wife.

From day one they took me in, a few were untrusting. They had experience and knowledge of things that were far in advance of my own. Imagine a 6 year old kicking a soccer ball around with an 11 year old, hanging out, no big deal. Some 67 year old man dates a 60 year old woman, that's great. The difference between 16 and 22 or 30 is a whole other matter as that age bracket as a whole is when a lot of people are just beginning to let loose.

The unknown issue was of course they all had seen, done and understood things 5 years or more ahead of me. Age was of no consequence to anyone and should not have been in that situation. I, at the beginning, felt as if I had to catch up and keep up to establish myself in whatever way, and I did, surpassing some at times.

Very infrequently there would be some ridiculous contest concerning who could drink more shots or drinks within a period of time. During one of my still teen birthday get togethers everyone present bought me celebratory drinks, all at the same time. The amount of drinks before me was laughable, and there was no measuring of liquor, all free hand pouring. As for the so called contests my usual response was bring it on, and it was brought on. I heard I was victorious at times, depending on ones' view of what victory is. In that case I guess alive would be sufficient.

I was truly the baby of the bunch, and from that time until now it didn't change, the wife almost 6 years older herself. It made me feel so special then and looking back I wouldn't change anything. The acceptance was akin to being knighted considering the popularity each had already attained before my arrival. The issues that followed were the results of bad decisions.

The apparel at this new job was whatever the hell you woke up in assuming work was acceptable that day. Almost all had their own music playing in their work area and it was especially prevalent in my zone. I had a broad exposure to music at this point but now I was hearing Gen-X, The Ramones, Sex Pistols and the like and I was as always taking it in. Oh, and pot, yes there was lots and lots of pot. Lots. A whole lot, which in little time would serve only as the appetizer.

Within two weeks of me starting there was a group of four or five that began to call me "Jet" for some reason. I paid little attention, just thought it was an inside joke. Day after day that name grew and latched on to everyone and became my identity there. Thereafter it became how I was introduced to any and all. I was comfortable with it, never knew how it came about and didn't care really. Soon I was Jet only, at work and otherwise and I welcomed it. It was my name and mine alone, Brandon was gone and good riddance. I was Jet, no last name needed. I would become someone else literally and my birth name would very rarely be used again to this day. Over time I met and befriended people who never knew my birth name even after 10 or 15 years. With my new identity I was king shit of turd island.

These crazies became my crew and as we continued working together we began also to spend much time together off the clock. Alcohol was a very common denominator for us with the exception of Tequila. It seems some of us had a shared allergic reaction to it whereas every time we drank it we broke out in handcuffs. The other spirits flowed freely accompanied by the weed and hash and quite frankly our noses could never be packed enough, we loved that shit. I had a fake ID for some time allowing me into many bars and other venues but was carded rarely. Those who actually did card me, they do bare at least some responsibility. At a little under 6 feet tall and 180 lbs., I really don't resemble a 6.5 ft. Hindu person.

So a long strange journey was starting that would lead to much excess, fuzzy memories and very tight knit friends. There were blinking red and blue lights occasionally and escorts to exits from places, but not for violent reasons, just clownish activities. I have wondered many times how the hell we got home or actually where we were, and who is this person next to me?

Undoubtedly we stepped on some toes, at times the whole foot. There were times that no one knew whos' toes or exactly what upset that person. One morning, having just woken up and still in-between worlds I felt something odd as I was stretching out. I leaned up and looked over to see some white, pasty dust like material going right across the sheet. When I turned to get out of bed for a better look there was another surprise. A small hole in the wall adjacent to the bed. It didn't take long to figure it out. Someone had shot through that wall, the white powder was from the sheetrock and the bullet had lodged into the bed frame about six inches away from pay dirt.

The one who fired the shot was visited by authorities eventually and taken away. He could deny firing any weapon and I'm sure he did. He could not explain however the vast amount of stolen items in his possession. The actual gun scenario was deemed unimportant and that was that. After things settled I began to realize that my very existence was due to a hardwood bed frame and a span of six inches. Of course I would come to know later, a blessing from above.

Sometimes we just live and refuse to learn. During one road trip to God knows where my pilot and I were smoking a joint, doing about 65 or so on the interstate as an 18 wheeler came along side of us. Apparently when we first passed him he had seen what we were doing. This guy was smiling, holding his forefinger and thumb to his mouth as if toking which made us laugh because we were stoned. What would idiots do? Unbuckle, lean out of the window, my entire torso, and attempt to pass the damn thing to the trucker. He is inching ever closer, of course much more elevated than our car. We did indeed pull it off back and forth for probably 2 miles. I am so fortunate, any subtle movement from either vehicle or bump in the road could have easily been the end. That particular day however we knew the guy appreciated it and we felt a kind of accomplishment as in getting away with something. The big picture remains, a couple of buffoons managing to avoid a gruesome death, live another day and blissfully unaware otherwise.

We were taking life by the horns and I suppose felt invincible. Our excursions were very fly by night and typically unsafe. We ventured into caves that were pitch black, feeling the way forward as far as possible not knowing what might be in there. When we ran across snakes, spiders or sometimes something furry and unknown we hurt our own selves trying to escape. Upon waking a bat colony, that's different. Lay flat, cover up as much as possible, hands over your head and wait. It was pretty clear when all of them evacuated and we could breathe deep and laugh.

We took coolers and certain other supplies into world class white water rapids where we knew others had died, drinking and such the whole trip. As I recall during the first trip we were enjoying shots of bourbon while gathering our supplies together at 7:00 a.m., the breakfast of champions. The somewhat calm beginning was helping to cure a few hangovers and also misleading as to what was ahead.

The ones who started ahead of us were about 300 yards downstream and it quickly became obvious they were getting into serious, heavy rushing water. As we were watching their raft would disappear behind a wave, reappear seconds later but only the front or rear could be seen. It became a water rollercoaster and there was no stopping it. We knew our turn was coming and coming quick.

The advice from one of the guides did get attention quickly before we could hear no more. As we approached the heavy rapids he yelled out "if we flip or you fall out try to swim to...," that's all I heard. The rushing was so loud and our raft was taking a heavy beating. Picture a raft large enough to easily hold 10 adults plus 3 or 4 coolers, then add the weight of the raft itself, had to be right at 3000 lbs. The water was so intense it would bend the raft almost in half despite the weight. I heard the words flip and swim, I knew the guide had to give such advice but it was irrelevant. Those rapids were moving so fast with so much power anyone overboard wasn't going to swim anywhere, rather end up wherever the water took them and hoping not into a giant jagged rock. His words also meant that a flip was a possibility which quickly became reality. As we paddled for our lives I would glance to the rear only for a second and notice 1 missing, then another 2 seconds later. We did flip over a couple times and thank GOD we all managed to resurface, some 30 or 40 yards away from each other and flailing but safe.

When we realized the coolers full of beer had been strapped in securely and were safe we just hugged and cried. As we dug into our so called waterproof bags wondering about cigarettes or other things, they too had made it. The crying turned to wailing, what a blessing. After that relief we went looking for those missing. Obviously no one was truly missing, just releasing the beer they had rented. The power of mother nature is amazing and having gathered any other items after flipping we saddled up and did it again. I vividly recall a deep concern for several lady friends who were with us, especially after we took a spill. When I resurfaced it was my first effort to visually locate them. If anyone were to ask why do such a thing, because it's there.

One unforgettable evening I decided to visit a girl who was on vacation about 6 or so hours away, no problem. The forecast for her particular area was brutal, very strong storms with frequent lightening, hail and many warnings issued for tornado activity. When I considered everything and the risks I gassed up right away and headed out. It really wasn't me driving but my libido. Long story short the closer I got the worse things got. I had slowed down to maybe 35, the wipers couldn't keep up remotely and the car was being blown side to side like nothing. Every direction was pitch black and ominous, not a light to be seen anywhere. Out of nowhere something appeared at the end of the hood and all I heard was crunching, glass breaking, the car taking a severe beating and in full uncontrollable spin. I more or less tried to duck and simply ride it out which seemed like an eternity. The car finally came to rest with nothing but branches and twigs in my view. It was so quiet other than that heavy rain and thunder. I had no sense of direction or full understanding of what happened. Large tree branches had come through the windshield and broken off, thankfully on the other side. I started it back up and eased my way in whatever direction would allow and pulled through what must have been either 2 or 3 huge pine trees blown onto the highway and had been invisible within the pitch black. I could see now 3 or 4 other cars in ditches and mud holes that suffered the same. My wipers were gone, headlight and grill destroyed, windshield smashed up, passenger side mirror missing, completely torn up. There were no emergency vehicles and likely none coming soon so I just continued on slowly, head hanging out to see and did get there. All for a girl.

She was glad to see me and for me such a welcome sight. I was such a nervous wreck by that time I could barely get her shirt off. She was worth the risk and I can think of no other I would have risked things for at the time. Maybe Jennifer Aniston. I suppose Angelina Jolie would have been a consideration but no one else. Probably.

There were race tracks where we traveled 180 mph inches away from the retaining wall, other cars even closer front and back. Not so much as a hint of braking on anybody's part. There were areas where you couldn't go left, definitely not right, if you slowed down you'd get rammed from behind, no choice but to maintain position and speed until an opportunity came. If there was a flat tire issue or mechanical problem, I guess just hang on tight and ride it out, that is where the excitement of the unknown kicks in. So close and fast, had anything happened to the car 10 places ahead it would have affected everyone behind. Later as I was reliving the experience I recalled how we all were required to wear helmets, made sense at the time. After the extreme close encounters however I thought, if something had happened at those speeds while we were inches apart, the only real purpose of the helmet would be to make it easier to pick up our detached heads. Wearing those helmets made about as much sense as getting into the ring with Mike Tyson thinking it'll be ok, I've got my mouth guard in. I believe we made plans for the next visit that same day.

We loved our guns like parents would children and made frequent trips to various places to not only target practice but also just blast, no targets needed. Sawed off shotguns, semi autos, more pistols than a licensed dealership, and believe me the girls loved it just as much. At times when it had snowed or was just brutally cold, no problem. We would make a fire, place our beer and other liquids in any given area to remain cold and burn a car tire that someone had acquired somehow. Tires burn a very long time and one learns quickly to be upwind.

In one particular outing we were done with shooting and looking out at the beautiful snowy landscape decided it's time enjoy the snow. We had positioned ourselves at the highest point we could reach for sledding purposes. Not just any sled would do though, we had the hood from some 1960's car, the whole damn thing. Six could fit on it easily, and did. The snow was dense, frozen on top and of course the hood was polished metal made into the perfect shape for such stupidity, aerodynamic. There is always a sense of excitement when traveling 50 mph on a car hood into darkness on a sheet of ice, knowing there's no stopping until the land levels or you hit something. One must think these things through and my thought was to sit behind the fat people, hell they were going to create the front end speed anyway. How that hood got there I have no clue, tire as well.

Not too long after the hood sledding adventure we visited a bar somewhere that had the mechanical bull ride available if one chose to dare. When the women would attempt they looked as if it came natural to them. The bull moving up and down, slightly side to side while the young lady held on. Anyone who has ever witnessed that has to admit it just straight up resembles sex, girl on top riding it out kicking ass sex. I only speak the truth.

Well my friend Jack (Daniels) convinced me to give it a try, what could happen? What I didn't know at the moment was the young ladies typically go on about speed dial 2, nice and easy. Apparently they cranked mine to 13 and after 3 seconds it looked like I was the bull's mistress, taking it hard while everyone else laughed and laughed. I'm quite sure it was funny at the moment.

Parties, drugs, alcohol, girls and music was a never ending pursuit, carried out mannerly and respectfully. Two of my co-conspirators had been dating girls now in college, of which there were several within 2 or 3 hours drive, meaning road trips! Let me say the crazy stories and rumors associated with some colleges are true, but crazier. I've been to many of those gatherings at several different campuses and what I observed was behavior just as crazy as ours only paid for by the parents. I saw kegs empty and full lined down sidewalks, tennis courts transformed into party central, people hanging off balconies, frat signs everywhere. These were good kids, polite and welcoming and there was just a sea of girls in any direction you looked, acting as if the world was going to end soon. I cannot imagine how some of them graduated.

Sometimes just to be assholes we would ask a local for directions somewhere and then claim they were lying after they told us, the funny part being they would then question their own selves about directions they just gave and beckon someone else to assist them, only to get the same response from us. It was funny at that time because on campuses one expects a good degree of intelligence which was there but sarcasm and real interaction outside the classroom they hadn't fully absorbed yet. I also fondly remember in one particular setting the girl to guy ratio at the time was about 4 to 1 and our ears were pinned back like dogs on the prowl.

One beautiful warm evening we visited several different frat houses and each one offered more alcohol and lunacy than the last. Following that were the clubs and bars. At one of the local haunts we began hearing about a party in this direction and one in that direction, but I had already focused on 2 or 3 girls living it up and developed tunnel vision. I said "you guys go ahead, I'll catch up" to which one of my buddies jokingly said "there is no I in team", as in stick together. I said "no there isn't but there are three u's in shut the fuck up," we laughed and split up. Some time later I was made an honorary member of the Zeta Tau Alpha fraternity and received a pledge pin in fact. I know some will say it couldn't be true, that's a female fraternity. That much is correct, all female indeed just not that particular night. I would also add that the girls kept a very nice, clean house if it makes the parents feel better. In all truthfulness those kids knew how to party and they did it continuously with no drama. Lots of puke and plastic cups but no drama, we loved them.

Around our stomping grounds things kept rolling along, we acted as if we had no upbringing most times and we were certainly known. On most party nights one phone call would initiate the plans followed by subsequent calls to others, everyone wanting to know where the crew was heading. Who had the coke and how much? Has anyone been to the ABC store yet? Who's picking up who and when?

No offense to the ladies but not once did any of the guys ask what another was going to wear or if a pair of jeans made his ass look big. It's the women who torture themselves by asking those questions, whatever the answer may be is wrong or speculative, just pretend it wasn't asked. There were times I wanted to respond with "no they don't make your ass look big, it's your big ass that makes your ass look big"!! Had I not been thinking about stroking that ass later, perhaps. On that topic, why would women want to be having a conversation in the bathroom while another was blowing out Mexican food from the previous night? Never understood it but apparently it's some kind of ritual.

Women and some of their doings were only outdone by us cave men and the stories of conquest. Some men, after a few drinks would have you believe they wrestled and defeated a bear, was a CIA operative, killed 627 men in battle with a spoon but most importantly...they say their penis is so big it has a knee in it. There are women out there however who think "well I bet it was a small bear, but how about we talk about that knee thing."

Then there were the followers of our campaigns who heard from sources where to be and when. Honestly it was considered fortunate in a strange way to be associated with our coven by some, not because we were special, we were not, but we had certain connections or other ways of getting into places, hearing about private gatherings or obtaining tickets to events for example. Those types of things were rarely free and sometimes those who missed out were wiser and better off.

The craziness continued as did the consumption, in cases we stepped over our own lines which was bizarre but we were humanish after all. Sometimes we would actually take 2 days off and drink water or tea to our livers' surprise. We were well acquainted with who to reach out to concerning our wants and needs, cocaine was now the drug of choice by far which only fueled our adventures. There were times of course when we went empty handed and those times were unpleasant.

There came a time when a friend of mine was about to be married and I, of all people, was asked to organize a bachelor party. I don't know why the powers that be thought I was the best or safest pick but in that circumstance one really can't say no. They knew me and my nature well enough and it sounded like a fun challenge so I said "well I'll see what I can come up with." I wasn't asked to do such again.

I knew of the perfect place very close by, a decent sized venue with a full hidden kitchen, a bar area, nice plush furniture, lots of large tinted windows and also a good sized stage or dance area in the middle. There was a nice paved parking area, outside tables and importantly it was secluded just enough to not bother others. I secured the place and began working on the fun stuff.

Having reached out to a few I began making phone calls to a much larger city about 2 hours away, a city known for that 'anything goes' lifestyle. I explained my dilemma along with what my initial thoughts were and in short time had reserved what was appropriate for the occasion. Two young beautiful ladies who would travel to us and entertain. I think now I might have been a little hasty, at least gotten some details or specifics. After hanging up I recalled seeing some 'working girls' in the past that were slightly unattractive. To be blunt, their head and/or face area looked like their neck threw up, it's a rough life. That would not be the case for this event thankfully. I was maybe 23 at the time and that level of detail never entered my mind. There was no asking google, things of that nature so I got lucky even before the event.

When the evening came everything was coming together as planned. The guests were arriving and ready to go, the groom had been delivered and of course the beverages had been planned out well in advance. I can't do everything by myself so a few others had been dispatched to handle the more private party favors and they had done well. For the first 2 hours or so it was simply all about the groom. Laughing, joking, rubbing elbows and getting more and more enjoyable. Then it was time for the girls.

They arrived only a few minutes late, no big deal and were accompanied by a fairly large gentleman as a type of security. Considering they're specific expertise we understood, ushered them inside so they could freshen up and pay homage to the groom.

These two young women were as one would expect and when the exited the vehicle there was no disappointment. Both very fit, somewhere between cute and hot, dressed for the occasion but again nicely. I suppose it goes with the territory but the perfume and makeup were in my view a little heavy, then I realized this is an ass show not a fashion show. The show must go on.

The girls began by dancing around the perimeter, speaking to all they passed, then came the inevitable lap dances which were highly impressive.

To our surprise the girls began to kiss lightly, then full on tongue sucking and almost immediately what little they had worn was gone, completely. They laughingly asked others for some space on that little dance floor, exchanged hand holding for hugging and within a few seconds, began to vividly show the group just how very much they liked each other. There's no need for specifics in the matter, the fact is they really really liked each other to a very high degree and happily showed it, for some time. The whole scenario had come about so fast that it took a few minutes for a couple of us to get our thoughts together.

The room was only lit to a degree, the clothes were off in a flash and the rubbing, kissing and licking between the two had given them a more everyday average appearance. How so? Whatever blush, eye liner and lipstick each had applied earlier was somewhat gone, transferred to the other ones' breast area, stomach and thighs. A couple of us began to think or contemplate...these two young ladies were just that, young. Perhaps a little too young, I personally thought 17ish or so. There was no way of knowing or certifying beforehand, really no way to know for sure at this juncture now. Their act was well into the final stages, it was also a bachelor party and just as important we could very well be wrong, we simply were unsure, guessing. At the stage they had progressed to it was about impossible to have a readily available ID on their person should anyone ask, which was not even a consideration. There were only 2 or 3 of us having that question, the remainder of the guys carried on as they should have, never giving it a thought. We were probably wrong and that's what we have to go by. It was just one of those "oh shit" moments very briefly.

The night went on with no fear of running out of supplies, tons of fun and as one might imagine with 25 or so drunken half-crazy young men things got a little messy. A few of us would return in the morning to make it all spic and span, simple. Things did not quite turn out that way.

The following day when we arrived with the best intentions we were greeted by a lady who was a little upset. More like pissed, actually furious beyond control. She was walking towards us screaming, yelling, absolutely going berserk and pretty close to foaming at the mouth. She called us heathens, animals, sons of bitches, idiots, more names than any of us had ever been called in one sitting. She said we'd shit in the floor, pissed on the sofas, puked all over the place, destroyed everything. On my word none of that was true, none. We had maybe a squirt cheese fight, thrown some sausage or other small edibles at each other's mouths, spilled a cooler and some drinks, probably ate without the benefit of plates. Those things were uncalled for yes, but her accusations were not true. Her last remark to us was that police had been called and were on the way. That's all we needed to hear and evacuated immediately taking every side street available. None of us heard another thing about it. Seems a fake ID can provide more than alcohol.

It was apparent that my crew was well known at about every watering hole in town. We sometimes had access to back doors or side doors and at times gained entry to places well after closing, we might have offered treats to do so but no problem. There were rarely issues with others and if so we had a small army that consisted of brothers and friends of people I had known but didn't really know them personally. It does make one feel good in any event. I know now we weren't that special, it was just the hour at hand at the moment. It some way it felt comforting, perhaps too much when people would approach me in any given party atmosphere and hug, ask you to meet others, pats on the back yet the whole time I had no idea who that person was.

The music environment had been heavy for some time and I was involved as I could be. Oddly enough I sang for a band once which was not my strength musically speaking but no one threw cans at me. Nor bras. I could sing on key but it wasn't my desire, I wanted to drive the band forward with percussion. My place was behind the scenes, behind those beautiful drums and surrounded with cymbals, my comfort zone.

I did have the experience of recording in an actual studio once, songs and lyrics of our very own. Simply amazing and eye opening, actually getting first hand visuals of how things are done, of course not at the highest level. Guitars would record the first tracks, then bass, sometimes together. I would come along and fill in which was odd as usually the tempo was coming from me. Everything I had was equipped with microphones and dampeners, headphones on. One little miscount or misstep was easily picked up so there was a little pressure. We knew what we were capable of and pulled things off pretty quickly minus a little editing later. I play that CD often even now and I'm not ashamed at all, the music speaks for itself. Commercially it was nonexistent but that doesn't speak for the result. There were clear areas where improvements would have made differences. For example, due to time constraints and expenses I wasn't allowed to set up and use my kit, I had to use the studio set. I had to make certain changes concerning height and distance, the quality and actual sound was not mine but I worked with it. Asking a drummer to do that is like asking a guitarist to play on some other guitar they don't know. There's no feeling for it. Had some producer said to Eddie Van Halen "we don't have a lot of time, how about you play this guitar instead?" Anyone who knows what I speak of knows. That's just a part of being a drummer. All in all the experience was great, not a lot of people can say they've been there.

One of the more memorable events was playing an outdoor venue, a biker rally that had been organized by a well-known biker gang that shall remain unnamed. From an outsiders point of view it might have been confused as a knife show or leather convention, not to mention the many, many beautiful bikes. To be clear there were lots of knives and acres of leather.

The area covered more than several football fields dotted with beer tents and grills, tents and small campers on the outskirts by the dozens, and a nicely placed stage complete with an overhead cover. A little intimidating at first glance considering all of the rebel flags and more than enough pointers as to who was in charge. They came to party pure and simple. I don't know how we got that gig, I only assume it's because we were a rock band and rock only. God forbid we had started a set with Boy George or something.

When we got to the stage we were greeted by several people who eagerly helped unload the heavy amps and stands, putting things into place as directed. As far as cabling, miking and that sort of thing we were fairly picky and no help was needed. I'll not forget that as we continued to get the equipment set it was made verbally clear, over the microphone, that no one was to approach the band at all, don't speak to them, and we were to have whatever we needed. From that point on we felt completely safe and we truly were.

When people use the term "raising hell" it was personified at this event! They raced bikes through fields, girls wrestled each other in the mud, people were being pulled behind bikes using chains wrapped around tractor tires, complete insanity that never let up in every direction. Beer was flowing like the Mississippi after 4 days of rain and no matter where a head turned women were flashing their tits at a rate faster than one could take in, some I wish I had not seen. There's no question a lot of the girls had that party, care free sexy mystique that drew you in. There were a few however that when they did expose their tits, the armpits were so hairy it looked like they had Bob Marley in a headlock. The bikers yelling "show your tits" while I'm thinking please no. As opposed to yanking a shirt down from the collar area to expose themselves, a few could have simply lifted the bottom of their shirt from the waist upward. They wouldn't have needed to go any further than just above the belly button.

They provided us with food, drink, privacy, anything we needed, and as one would imagine all cash afterwards. The lifestyle is certainly not one most would choose, but in the end they were just people, very open and honest no room for doubt people. The women seemed particularly proud of their breasts judging by the apparent hatred of bras, or in a few cases a hammock might have been more appropriate. We never saw any fighting or hints of trouble at all to which I'm grateful because those guys could cause a lot of suffering and without hesitation. Hell the women looked as if they'd served in the navy during Guadal Canal, spoke like it as well, but funny as hell and we loved it. I have to say I felt more comfortable that afternoon then I have in some bars.

I had also met with another group a few times, a brotherhood, they were not bikers nor the KKK but they had certain ideals and standards to live by. I had been employed once in a way that put us in the same vicinity a few times and the talk was always relaxed and pleasant. I had seen them in their street clothes with the many tattoos showing, also I'd seen them dressed very sharply as if going to a formal event. In that regard they looked like a well-dressed co-worker or just someone to pay no attention to. Judgements of others are commonly wrong, they could have mingled with any high society group, probably have. Additionally the ones I dealt with were very well spoken, very mannerly and to themselves. They were not highly known of in the area, by their design I suppose. They were clearly known by the powers that be outside of the area however, why I can't say. Very large, muscles on top of muscles, strong as oxen and not to be crossed by anyone, including the bikers. They wanted to remain under the radar and succeeded in the effort. Why others go poking around, asking questions or starting rumors is beyond me. Bottom line, mind your business, no problems. I had heard of the fate a few had suffered due to their own mouths or simply not willing to walk away when given the chance. I'm confident in saying it was a one-time mistake.

So why did the musician cross the road? Because he heard the chicken was a slut. For whatever reason guys in bands girls and partying have been synonymous, drummers having the worst reputation. I suppose it must have been similar in the 1700's but that come on had to be brutal. "Sir thou makest me desire things better unspoken, wouldst thou care to tame my speech with thine masculinity?" I'd be like "I don't know what the Hell you just said but you're turning me on, maybe I can throw a beer down your throat and give you a ride? If it makes better sense I mean tappeth thine hindquarters".

I wasn't always propositioned but some band girls did make things easy. During a set break one night I noticed this young lady sitting alone at the bar, she had been dancing earlier, and she was hot. We said our hellos and talked maybe three minutes when just out of nowhere she said "you wanna go fuck?" I have to say I did like the approach and bluntness but damn. Playing hard to get was something she just did not care for. I had to play another set in minutes so it didn't transpire. Later I heard that she was crazy, bordering on psychotic and had a couple of restraining orders against her from previous boyfriends who were currently healing. Beautiful and crazy as hell simultaneously, I dodged that one but still remember that invite, very impressive. Another example of something, someone watching over and giving me the fortitude to walk away. I couldn't help but think what it might have been like to have nasty throw down pickle in the mouth sex with a gorgeous psychotic she wolf. She truly could have been the cover of Playboy in my view, or maybe the cover of Playdead.

Then there was the girl who had seen the band a couple of times, really cute lean and very fit. I later learned she was a dance instructor which means to a guy she could be a human sex pretzel, bend and mold Gumby. She was aggressively flirty, sometimes a person just knows without question what's happening. We just began shooting the shit one day when she asked if I had a pen to which I obliged and she proceeded to write down her name and number. The chemistry was unquestionable to the point of let's just fuck and get to know each other later. She also left the sweetest message of how we should be friends, and just how inexplicably friendly she wanted to be... over and over. It was truly an offer not available in stores. I couldn't dance, she couldn't play drums, but we had that one thing in common that snares many, alcohol. Not that it was needed in her case but it does babysit your brain while your self-control is getting an ass whipping. Sometimes when some very desirable person had made their nasty intentions known and then followed through, the timing might've been off.

At times I might find myself with someone bizarre as I came out of a fog or whatever, looking for the courage to say "I'm gonna give you 25 minutes to stop". I just couldn't bring myself to it and potentially hurt their feelings after all the effort and care they had expelled. I'm just a big ole softie. The five words I always loved hearing as a drummer were "what are you doing later?" The more frequent words were "will the defendant please rise." It goes with the territory.

I had practiced and played for years, not just percussion but I knew the key strokes in any particular song we played, the lyrics, crescendo and decrescendo. As I progressed I subtly added little inserts and offbeat intricacies that most wouldn't even notice but the very little details I loved. I had paid particular attention to a few of my personal favorite drummers and their unique styles. The studying, reading and constant listening truly paid off because I had become comfortable with power drumming as well as the lighter finesse type, lots of off counts and accessories. Now I realize it was my escape from reality. The world I was in was far from a reality known by most. Of course I enjoyed the playing, practicing and learning but I never gave much thought to the fact that I had no worries in those hours, no stress, bad stuff went away. It's so very easy to see when one takes the blinders off.

We played certain things that were typically hard to perform in a live setting so most other bands wouldn't even attempt to. That gave us just a little more appreciation from the crowd and venues, especially those who knew music. It also made us better individually. In my personal opinion the fewer members in any given band dictate a higher level of expectation and performance. On the other hand, bands that had 2 or more guitarists, some brass or keyboards and extra percussion would blow my mind.

I had been approached several times to teach children of some who attended some of the shows and it truly was an honor to be asked. I'm not teacher material and had to decline explaining that I was self-taught.

I could show them the basics and teach them the 4-4 count that creates a basic rhythm and such, how to tune etc... What I could not teach was fundamentals, sheet drum notes and all of the proper class techniques. There was no way in my view to explain what each foot is doing while both hands are doing something opposite. Then there was the potential worry of how or when to say to the parent maybe they might consider a tambourine or dart board. I only knew what I knew, almost impossible to pass on but again most flattering. If I were able to teach others properly I would have done so happily.

The parents that had asked for my assistance always approached me at the moment, meaning I was actually playing a gig and on break, or they would wait until we were done. I thought to myself after declining, they likely had no idea what they were asking. Unlike a stringed instrument percussion is not so easily turned down. There are dampeners yes, but they only work to a degree which usually does not coincide with the degree of which a parent wants to relax after work. The cost involved depends on the type of equipment and how far one is willing to go, either way very expensive. Being asked to teach in any capacity is a great compliment that confirms hard work etc...

Back to Assville, my friends and I knew that appearance was indeed a factor as we all appreciated. Times had changed quite a bit and one either rolls with the changes or gets left behind. The clothes, hairstyles, any materialistic things were becoming very high priority throughout society. I can say we did adapt quickly and in a lot of cases stayed ahead of the market. Not because we were fashion geniuses, we simply knew that our night lives and everything associated with them were in the eyes of others. We were never under pressure to do things we didn't care for or reverse who or what we were, much too late for that. We became very aware early on that that there was much competition for what we had already carved out for ourselves, the men on the prowl never ceased or relented, as if they were coming from some type of testosterone fertilizer. It was understood and we gave each other equal space as long as they didn't go too far in our haunts, as in being overly loud, obnoxious, maybe experimenting with claiming a table or spot known to be ours. There were discussions at times that were very brief, no altercations really. Those scenarios can be summed up easily with one word, pride. One of those deadly sins.

The girls, known or not, obviously were the main focus most evenings and they knew it, loved it, took full advantage of the attention. I do know it made each of them feel so good and attractive as it verified their 6 hours of bathroom makeup and never ending hair corrections. In all truth, seeing and knowing their enjoyment really made me happy whether I received any notice personally or not. I am no Adonis, I've really never been comfortable entirely with my mirror self and always tried to make any improvements I could. I don't have the appearance of one whose' face was on fire and put out with an icepick either, just average. The later an evening gets, a persons' looks are directly related to the alcohol consumption of the aggressor. There were one or two times when young ladies approached me clearly drunk and made their intentions unmistakable. Subtle little phrases that one might have to take a step back and read between the lines. Things like "I lost my keys damn it. I think I left them on your kitchen table." My favorite, "the food is really good here...you can grab my ass if you want to." Without the benefit of a pocket sized 'Drunken Jibberish to English' manual, a person is left to try to make sense of what the other is trying to convey.

Sarcasm aside, I knew when and if to take advantage of an invitation from someone who was in a decent frame of mind at the time. I'm confessing that on those occasions, knowing a particular girl was very drunk, I did not take advantage. I responded with some garbled trash talk and said I had to go be excused or something and would be right back. I was never right back, only in the shadows watching over the situation. I did the best I could also to make damn sure the girl did not even interact with a few certain people. As for those who did, and still do take advantage of others in a drunken or otherwise vulnerable situation, karma is a bitch.

As for physically fit I was as much in shape as I could be. The years of drumming had an effect from shoulders down, I did work out several times a week and had trained in martial arts a spell, so those hobbies were helpful in that regard. I was not as a Greek statue certainly, more of a decorative stone but my point is there was always competition on the playing field so one must be at least presentable, otherwise kicked to the curb and going home alone. Admittedly there were times going home alone would have been the smart, sober choice. I do know first hand when the crazy girls were on the prowl in those days a first visual impression often was the difference between waking up alone or waking up in a strange bed not alone. There were times where the first option would have been best but 6 hours earlier your penis was calling the shots, after several shots.

We carried on with ourselves and time went by as we met and mingled with many people, which eventually led to a special someone who would become my wife, partner, fun time any time girl and share many things with me, even other women.

We had met briefly before and mostly knew all the same people, she just had other things going on preventing her from going out frequently. She was an eye catcher for sure, green eyes, blondish mostly with a tint of some red. She had a very well sculptured frame but most inviting was her open mindedness, sense of humor and a great laugh. It was immediately clear we were both interested and as the night went on, drinks as well, we talked more and more and got closer and closer.

Eventually I decided to attempt to escalate things, by that time we were eyeballing each other constantly even if completely separated. I casually made my way back to her and her girlfriends and as she began to say something I just leaned in and kissed her, pushed my tongue in her mouth dead in front of everyone. She was truly surprised just as her friends were but I did not get pushed away, questioned or slapped. When our lips separated she just said "OK, alright then." That's how it all started, sometimes you just have to follow that instinct and at that time my instinct was her ass is going to be mine. Tonight. Apparently her instinct as well.

When things began winding down we made our way to her apartment and just through the door when the movie scene began. Pictures knocked off the wall, chairs shoved all over, the magazine rack never had a chance. We were going at each other like crazed wolverines trapped in a blender and the proof was evident when we saw the entry way the next morning. It was funny in a damn look what we did kind of way. I wasn't sure if to apologize, say thanks or just get right back at it. Eventually all 3 came to pass.

When the time came to leave we said our goodbyes and I made my way home, caring for some scratch marks and I know I had a grin which wasn't going away. I let the night remain as it was about 2 weeks before I could stand it no more and made that first call. She was happy beyond belief and we couldn't make plans soon enough. She had been concerned that maybe she had been a little too welcoming that night, silly girl. In hindsight it appears as if we were just supposed to be together, and we were from then on. I was her Mr. Right whereas before I was to others Mr. he'll do.

The magnetism was strong, we just couldn't keep our hands off of each other. We went at it anywhere, everywhere possible. Kitchen table, restaurants, bathroom, other people's bathrooms or kitchen tables, driveway, yard. Somehow we even managed the back of a big travel bus, fortunately for others we were seated in the back. In short time it just became a running joke for everybody else. Whenever we would go to a party or some get together the first words were "YOU TWO BEHAVE." The warnings really were ignored and people accepted it, with grins and gossip.

As time moved on and we were established as a certified couple we only intensified the bedroom activities. There were certain outfits or parts of outfits she enjoyed wearing and I welcomed also. Perhaps a small degree of restraint at times, other items as desired. We planned time for full evening long sessions with specific music, candles, a meal afterwards that had been thought out in advance. Typically it all started with a lengthy shower or bubble bath which set the mood. Times were not boring by any means, only becoming more adventurous.

After dating for some time I decided to ask her the big question, not if she had a twin sister but rather if she would marry me. I had already purchased the ring set, decided what night would be best and I stuck to the plan. She was so excited, happy, crying and hugging me, finally saying yes. When the big day came all was nice and simple, a pretty quick affair. We had reserved a clubhouse for that night for everyone to gather and celebrate with all the usual party favors of course. When we had enough of that we had a nice suite waiting where we would stay the night and honeymoon from there. That's where things got interesting.

When we arrived at the hotel we were feeling no pain, still excited and giddy. We took advantage of the shower, sofa, bed, desk area, balcony, pretty sure the elevator etc.. Finally, after all that excitement and celebrating we both collapsed and passed out. At some point she woke up thirsty, dying for a soft drink. There was no drink at that point so she had no option but to visit the vending area. In her fuzzy state of mind she decided to just dash to the machine area real quick, get a drink and run back. Naked. She cracked the door and peeked out, the coast was clear as it should have been at about 4:30 a.m...she took off with nothing but a wedding ring and a handful of quarters. She got the drink and turned to go back, immediately realizing she had no idea what room, room number, and in her state of mind wasn't even sure what side of the hall. At that point she froze in panic. Looking at one end of the very long hallway and then the other, all the doors looked exactly the same.

She began quietly, gently trying each door knob she came to, one after another when she heard a door abruptly close. Busted! Some guy had come out of his room at one far end of the hall looking as if he might be heading to some business meeting. When he turned he got quite a surprise. They locked eyes for a brief second and she quickly backed up to the first door she could as if she couldn't be seen. She really hadn't accomplished much, picture standing in front of your bathroom with the door closed. Between the door and wall is maybe 3 inches, that was her hiding place. Unless a person is skinny enough to walk through a harp that isn't going to work. I guess in his mind he didn't know if she was a victim of some foul deed and escaped or what. He said "ma'am, ma'am are you alright, do you need help?" At that very moment she saw our door, it wasn't latched closed. There was a very small gap between the door and frame with just enough light to give it away, so she took off and busted in, myself still asleep.

I suppose that set just a little bit of the tone of things to come, we had much in common. One huge commonality I would find out about was she had developed a curiosity and desire for another woman. Not as a separate situation, one who would join us to create a whole new dynamic. It had been her idea, her desire and something I never would have brought up myself. To make things even more interesting she was clear that another man was not an option, not even to be discussed. That was enormous because it was impossible from my perspective. She had tunnel vision on this new venture and wasn't going to let it go.

I will say the sharing thing is a fantasy never fulfilled with a lot of men and women both. Having been there many times it still remains fantasy like, especially since the whole idea was initiated by her. It irks me in some way, the wife felt likewise, that despite a persons' true desire not only would they hide and bury it but at the same time exclaim how unbelievably awful and disgraceful in their mind. At some point that same person had become aware of our inviting nature and almost had to be beaten away with a stick. I have zero patience for those who try to step on others only to elevate themselves, all the while doing everything humanly possible to erase all proof of the many phone calls made and discreet messages left.

I had heard at one point from some study done that about 75% of women (those part of the study) had fantasized about being with another woman yet highly unlikely to verbalize or initiate it. After the many times I was a witness and participant I have to agree. Hell if I was a woman I'd be so damn gay there would be journals written about me along with professionals studying my gayness. Then again, if I had 2 beautiful breasts I'd never leave home and starve to death eventually. Damn, as long as no one is being coerced or misled and nobody gets hurt just do what you gotta do. In the end, none of us are getting out of here alive.

As our talk continued she inquired about my feelings on the matter incessantly, must have asked me at least twice. After much thought, every bit of 2 or 3 minutes, I conceded. Being the gentleman I am and out of the kindness of my heart her wish to incorporate another young lady was agreed upon. Now not just anyone would do, the participant(s) had to be eye catching, uninhibited and care about their appearance overall. We were patient, selective and those ideals paid off greatly.

When we first began searching we somehow ran across an ad or something she had seen on the computer speaking of an upcoming large assembly in a nearby town. I can't say what the actual wording was but without doubt an assembly of swingers. They somehow, using whatever name, had rented the entire floor of a nice hotel and it was to be private. All we needed to do was register. I was thinking yeah I gotta see this. When the day arrived we were excited and giddy only wondering what to expect but not quite positive, we just wanted a hot girl and that's all we wanted.

We checked in and made our way to the room passing by so many people milling around talking and laughing with drinks in hand. As mentioned before they had rented the entire floor and every couple had their own room but every door was wide open. There was a large room at one end of the hallway that had been transformed into a nice bar area combined with a dance floor and social gathering tables. We bought a few drinks and met some people, slowly becoming at ease as person after person introduced themselves and made their interests very clear to us new kids.

We were surrounded in a sexual fog very quickly by men and women both, we weren't intimidated but kind of grinning and thinking "this is unreal". Every man and woman was hot on her ass, rightfully so. I got the same treatment, however my very strong but invisible vibe to the men was exuding from every pore...don't even think about it!

As time passed during the social gathering people began to get very comfortable and frisky. The touching and lite rubbing had begun along with kisses and tongues, we just observed. We decided to take more scenery in and exited the bar area into the main hall. It was immediately clear that every door to every room was propped wide open the entire length of the hall. Upon reaching the first room we could see four couples sharing the sofa and chairs in the small living area, two couples with the men on top and two with the women on top, all pounding like they were earning points. The next room offered two women laid across the small bar as two other women were having their oral way. Over to the left two more couples who appeared as if they were digging for gold, hammering away like someone dared the other. Similar scenes were repeated in every room and we were welcomed to come and go as we pleased. Joining in at any time was clearly welcomed. We obviously didn't know anyone and didn't care to in that situation. Far too open, far too blatant. The whole scenario was equivalent to some strange buffet. Some things look really good and enticing until you notice people in front of you grabbing things with bare hands, licking them and putting them back. Of course someone may get past that initially, then you get a good look at those hands.

My first thought personally was there must be 60 to 70 people here for this fuck fest. Clearly everyone didn't know everyone yet the willingness to swap DNA along with every damn thing else was not a concern, which indeed was a concern for us. We did not participate but proceeded to our room, door closed and treated each other disrespectfully but lovingly. Our mission was clear from the beginning, female only. Period. Eventually there was an open horny ear.

The wife had been discreetly sharing what had happened to a long time friend, not someone who was considered a regular but friend none the less. She wanted all the details and there was laughter along the way but she also had been harboring that same desire. Very sweet, not innocent by any means but not sleeping around everywhere either, we knew the background. We were already comfortable with each other from the past, throw in several drinks and shots combined with the swinger party discussion and within a half hour we were all three sitting on the bed kissing and laughing. Not long after the wife and I had her bra off and were in competition as to who could lick the most or get the first moan. The rest happened very quickly but the girls were comfortable together for sure and it was over relatively quickly. Not mind blowing or out of this world, but hell the worst sex I ever had was great. To put it another way there were three more occasions with her, no arm twisting needed but something was still kind of missing.

The second encounter had come about in a very unexpected way. It seems the wife couldn't contain her thirst for more and as women at times do, couldn't hold back what was supposed to be private. She shared what had taken place with a friend known to her since 2nd grade, a guy who knew her probably better than anyone. They never went out or dated but had always been more like siblings. A total shock and surprise was in store for sure, this guy was frequently out of the country with work obligations and his desire and that of his wife were that Lee and I would keep his wife company while he was away, keep her occupied and content. His only want was to hear the details later. In this particular circumstance I knew there would be no jealous spouse or bad feelings, hell he initiated it. It was a jaw dropping offer that we simply had to follow up on and the decision was made for myself, my horny wife and the lonely unknown wife to meet at a local bar, the plans had been set in motion.

When the time arrived it seemed like we had waited months. We arrived a little early to unwind and have a cocktail, both of us visualizing what may be coming. When she arrived there was a mutual sigh of relief. We had a general idea of what she looked like but an in person meeting is different. Without speaking it was clear our decisions were the same. YES. We care about your loneliness and we will help you. Over and over.

The interview process was simple...attractive, pleasant, friendly, breathing, and one must take into consideration she showed up knowing what the plans were, knowing she was on the menu and that says a lot. She was a little nervous, as were we but we all pushed that aside. Poor ole lonely empty house having big chested girl, our empathy was immediate and we knew we had to do the neighborly thing. It wasn't Mr. Rodgers neighborhood that's for sure.

After having a few cocktails and getting better known to one another we made our way to our residence, and there was no question as to what was to come, that was clear in advance therefore no need for intimate foreplay. Foreplay in that instance was something like "what's your cats name? let's fuck." I'm pretty good at reading in between the lines and I felt somewhat comfortable with saying "well, if it makes you feel better." I just felt like I needed to go that extra mile, of course I had the best copilot one could want. If I had taken the wrong exit or failed to yield she would be there saying floor it, somewhat like a crew chief might say. The level of comfort was amazing.

After some kissing and rubbing we moved on to a hot bubble bath with candles flickering everywhere as music played, and began to take each others clothes off. The tongues were going wild and landed wherever they landed while six hands were exploring any body part available. Hell I might have rubbed my own ass. Before we could step into the tub Miss lonely was on her knees with one hand grabbing Lee's ass and the other mine, and she proceeded to orally show her appreciation to us, taking turns back and forth. When I hear someone say "cut to the chase" there is no better definition. Too many details follow that intro but it was in the end exhausting and no regrets. We had two more meetings afterwards before things died down which had to happen eventually. The events with those hot girls had turned us into vampires by now, just thirsting for more but we would not, could not get complacent and just settle for a body as no one should. Enter Jackie, or as I referred to as "Jackpot."

One summer afternoon the wife had gone to a community pool, the type with a paid membership and had run across someone she'd recognized from long ago. A friend of this person and knows that person kind of thing and they talked the rest of that afternoon. When time came to leave they decided to come to our place to have a drink and hang out while waiting for me to get home. It turns out I knew of her as well as she did me but from some time ago. So there sat the two of them laughing and joking when I walked in and we were re-introduced, "Jet you remember Jackie right"? I said "yes I believe I do". I got comfortable and a few drinks later we were like long lost friends. When I went back to the restroom the wife came in behind me and looked me straight in the eyes and said simply "she's the one"...no questions or anything. She had a look of fantasy about her, a huge grin and she was in the womanly position to know, Jackie was the one. Who was I to argue?

Describing Jackie is akin to trying to describe a thunderstorm, so much going on. About five foot six with coal black straight hair almost to the waist and striking green eyes. Her body was amazing, her tits were the type that captivated you but not overly large, waist much smaller and the hips almost mirrored the chest, a work of art, I wanted to have her baby. As if all that weren't enough she could draw someone in with her personality and demeanor alone, laughing at everything and cussing like a sailor at times, very boisterous for sure. If it hasn't been made abundantly clear she was fucking hot to the point of one being or becoming out of self-control.

So there we are having cocktails, maybe some other party favors and it was so damn obvious, so clear what was on the agenda for the night. It's unknown still how Jackie knew but it was understood she knew precisely where we were heading as a trio and in retrospect she was maybe two steps ahead of us. The hungry for you now look was intentional and so damn powerful, head slightly down but eyes staring upward, first to me then the wife. The sexual chemistry had been building a bit and it wasn't long before it was dripping off the damn walls and pooling at our feet. I do not recall any nervousness or hesitation whatsoever from the two of them as we got closer and closer and the first kiss from me, then from the wife which automatically brought out Jackie's tongue to be met by hers. That little teasing continued maybe ten minutes and we could not nor did control ourselves from there.

One must truly visualize my perspective with eyes closed and total concentration. On one side the wife, green eyed blonde with her mouth just open enough to get more oxygen, breath heavy and ready to pounce. On the other this green eyed black haired vixen with a slight grin and lips wet as shit from the previous twenty minutes or so, our faces inches apart and eyes wide open. If Tarzan had been found by two naked horny centerfold models only he would really understand. It was erotic, electric and unstoppable.

We were each comfortable ready and able, hands going every direction but my feeling was to let the two get better acquainted and they wasted not a split second. They just looked at each other and in one swift move the wife moved forward and pushed her mouth on Jackie's open mouth and their lips met. The wife grabbed Jackie by the back of her head and thrusted her tongue seemingly down her throat, to be answered by Jackie reaching up to grab the wife's tits with a little attitude and began pulling and squeezing with both now making those sounds of "fuck me". I was brought into the mix very quickly, as in they both still had saliva from each others lips connecting themselves. The perfect storm had developed and was getting ready to unleash, the likes of which could not be imagined.

We started with a hot shower and went to one another like damn cannibals. If the situation presents itself a nice big bath or shower is a fantastic start, calming and relaxing and all are clean with water cascading off every body part. The wet skin and dripping wet hair was just an additive to the sounds being made and the uninterest as to who's arm or hand was whose. Full on contact with little shoves and grabs, hair being wiped out of faces and absolutely no room for shyness, it was a take no prisoners event. We never dried off or had use for a towel but continued until we reached the bed, thankfully a big bed.

Crawling onto that bed with hands full and mouths busy just didn't seem that difficult as we were helping each other a bit. The dim lights and instrumental music in the background was not even thought of at the time as their addition was perfect. The three of us were kind of reckless for a short time, rubbing and grabbing at will with each being equally attended to. Soon we began to get horizontal or relatively close and that act sent the message of do what the hell ever you want and so we did.

Scratching pulling and pushing was non stop, biting and a little slap here and there followed by some giggles. There are not enough pages or adjectives to explain what took place from then on but memories remain. Not one inch of skin went without a tongue or two tongues grappling for that area. We had shared everything from the tub to intense sensations, a lot of DNA and several physical marks. The only differences between that encounter and a full on XXX scene being filmed were the lack of cameras and pay. In the end we all were crumbled in a slippery pile and recovering. It was time for Jackie to go home so we hugged and said our goodbyes which was sort of sad. As we talked about what had transpired Lee expressed she hadn't experienced everything she wanted in a three hour session, no complaints whatsoever but wanted more. The next encounter was being planned within one hour of the last and good ole Jackie felt the same. We set the date for the first availability for all, the next night.

As the following evening got closer we got more and more excited as a result of thinking of what had already happened in comparison to what may be, Jackie was in the same boat we would learn later. As usual we started with some drinks and other things as the music played, laughing and bullshitting for a while. The comfort level on our first night was wonderful for all but within those few after hours it became exceptional, we knew damn good and well what was coming and who, just not when.

It began kind of nasty flirty with little comments about whose tongue was where the night before followed by comparing bite marks and such. The first tongue and kiss was lightning fast behind that and suddenly it was if things never ended. Round two was just a bit more uninhibited.

We went straight to the shower, kissing and mouthing along the way only this time each took what clothes remained off personally. Into the shower, a little steam visible as the door opened and again we pulled each other tight and grabbed body parts as if the world might end. The night before was damn nasty and etched into memory, this night would be lewd and sleazy. There was a built in half shelf that went around the circumference of the shower for soaps and such that also worked well for a foot rest.

Strict details may be a little much, just picture Lee and Jackie in a sex driven staring contest. Is it possible to sweat in a shower? So the first hour had passed bringing on the next three or four which did prove just as loving so to speak. Honestly another shower was needed, for actual bathing.

From that point on none of us could get enough and situations got more indescribable. One of the strongest grips was the language used, appropriate for the task at hand. Phrases like "tell me what to do Jet" or "pull my fucking hair bitch" were fairly common. "Hey, how was your day and take your clothes off while you answer", one of my favorites. When a person drags their ass in from a hard day of work only wanting to relax, well that thought goes away quickly.

We rented hotel rooms, missed days from work occasionally and sometimes were together three nights in a row. It was pure hedonism and straight filth by most accounts, we eventually were a trio well over thirty times, possibly forty. Every passing menage was more brazen and filthy than the last, to the point one would just ask for forgiveness in the morning.

In the otherwise real world we see or interact with others having that same mind set almost daily and never have a clue. Grocery stores, parent-teacher meetings, churches, restaurants, maybe even Wal-Mart. There are those that see another and wonder, contemplate, fantasize but rarely take that nervous first step and say "HI".

Conversely there are hints that point to no, not today, as in someone with mismatched flip flops, and socks no less, oversized pajama pants and the remnants of a t-shirt, on backwards, that exposes bra straps begging for relief, whipping some kids ass in aisle 14 while she cusses at somebody on her $900 phone for everyone other person to hear. Might want to let that one pass on by!

There are other pitfalls as well, one of the most dire being human nature in the form of developing strong feelings for such a long term partner which did happen.

As things got more developed and lustful we inevitably started having those feelings, one for another from all three angles. The wife and I became a little distant and argumentative, as did the trio as a whole. Inevitable I suppose having shared so damn much for so long.

Any thoughts of jealousy or perhaps leaving one partner out of an experience was a death sentence. I suppose it would be considered expected concerning the duration and intensity of our days and nights together, but unforgiving either way.

Jackie had made it clear to me she wanted an alone session which most certainly would not have been a one time thing. In one instance she asked what time I might come home for my lunch break so that she could be there to blow me like never before, something that I would not forget! Those were her words. The thought poisoned my mind with possibilities and just wanting to say yes. She had also propositioned the wife with the same idea to meet for some afternoon delight and her thought process was identical to mine. Jackie's magnetism and uninhibited nature were almost unbeatable. In fact it took the two of us to combine our individual fortitude and decline those offers. We patched things up quickly and the whole sordid affair was over, sad in some ways but very necessary.

There was no way that either of us could forget certain things nor did we want to. The flashbacks alone were enough to cause partial daydreaming and the desire for a cigarette. Jackie faded away but the memories absolutely did not. She had left an unmistakable mark on both of us as we had to her.

We did not pursue any more questionable sexual activities after that, at least none involving a third party. We had received what we wished for and quite a bit more.

Our lives continued on as regular lives would, we weren't lacking any attention or affection between the two of us as a now traditional couple. The partying and good times had not faded, our good friends as loyal as ever and we made newer friends as well. On occasion it seemed as if the only reason needed to celebrate was the grass had been mowed or somebody waved. We attended great concerts and professional sports events, shared vacations and just once in a while a jail cell.

Having been known to certain people does pay off once in a while. As I was mentally preparing myself for a short jail stay the thought always becomes what's going to happen, will there be trouble? As I was led in I was a little surprised to see a very large community type cell, at least a dozen beds but no one was there. I saw some personal items and clothing but couldn't figure it out. After a short time doors began to open and I heard multiple voices heading my way. I had a sudden realization, everyone had been out on work release. Now my mind is wondering if I unintentionally invaded someone's space or worse made myself comfortable on a bed claimed long before my arrival. If so, that's the kind of thing some take very personally, and not easily forgiven.

I walked towards the shared restroom and shower area so as to let them settle in, then I might be able to determine what was available and what was not. Suddenly someone called my name and as I turned I recognized the ragged looking face of one of my heathen friends from the older neighborhood. What a welcome and surprising sight. Not shocking by any means, very welcome though. Had he not been there I would have stood out like dirty underwear on a clothesline.

Joy and sorrow come hand in hand and so we also suffered together. We had lost several loved ones, some not a shock due to health issues, some very much unexpected. Of course we also were aging and that process began to show.

Clearly I picked up some bad habits during my journeys and the time came for me to admit some weaknesses and reach out, in this case alcohol. Of course I had been drinking since 13 or 14 years of age but that consumption grew as I did. Throughout my earlier years of drugs and alcohol I still exercised and worked out, was a regular member at a fitness club and otherwise cared for myself. I suppose ever so quietly and slowly my alcohol intake had multiplied much and now was out of hand. I ate little, didn't care to see anyone, hands shaking. To put things in better perspective I was such a regular at the ABC store that eventually I was given credit, as in "just pay me tomorrow" which had come about due to a card reading issue. Hearing those words was, I'd like to say "sobering" but that's not the best adjective considering. When credit is given at an ABC store there is likely a problem. Time for rehab and so I did just that.

After discussing all of my multiple disorders with people in that business it was determined I would go to a facility a few hours drive away for a 30 day stay. I did need it and they were agreeable to my cigarette smoking which could have been a concern so off I went, driving unknown roads and actually enjoying it. I suppose the beautiful fall weather did help keep my mind occupied while looking at the beautiful scenery. As I got closer the roads and town itself got smaller and smaller, very rural. The actual facility was a little dated, brick and about 3 stories with 2 wings stretching out from the main entrance. Funny thing is it was directly in the middle of a residential neighborhood, there were small houses on all 4 sides in very close proximity. I started thinking what one might say if trying to sell such a property..."well our neighbors are always trying to help people out, and we're right next door to the Crystal Methodist church."

After parking my car for the next 30 days I slowly headed to my cleansing, a little apprehensive and honestly watching, studying every movement and gesture of anyone I saw. The very first words I heard upon arrival came from a young guy asking if I had a cigarette, which I didn't really like. In my mind there must be 30 or 40 people here, if I give him one what about everybody else? Being new on the scene and as he was alone I gave him one and proceeded to check in. I would learn later some were there ordered by the court and had restrictions, others were like me, being voluntary and could leave any time. I can only assume the poor guy had no cigs and no options.

The facility itself was quite dated but nice for a bunch of lost people. The very first place I learned about was the pharmacy room, a very limited access area where pills were handed out throughout the day to help us poor souls not relapse or get medieval. Men and women obviously had separate hallways, 2 or 3 to a room but did not always stay away from one another, there were more than a few hookups.

As one would expect there were multiple daily classes dealing with dependency, emotional issues and the like and I never missed one. The rule of the house was before one could speak or respond to something that person first had to say "my name is so and so and I'm an alcoholic" or whatever the addiction was, then continue with the conversation. That was required before the person could actually begin to share whatever thoughts they had, every class every time. I hated it, never agreed with it and never will. They say it promotes accountability, well each person is there in the flesh, on stage and has already admitted their addiction, in other words being accountable. Many of those held quite a bit of shame because of their past but still had to say those words multiple times every day in front of everyone and the grief always remained.

I did see multiple people who just would not attend the classes any more only to become vegetable like in their room. Consider this..."Hi my name is Luke and I used to masturbate 27 times a day..." How many times should poor ole Luke have to be disgraced? Isn't it enough that his right arm is 3 times the size of his left?

From the start I was very open about my situation and was understanding of my new friends and the traps they had been snared in. A few alcoholics, some there for prescription meds but the majority was there for meth or anything related to it. There were kids high school age, moms and dads, college graduates, professionals and a few in their retirement years. We were all alike in regard to seeking a little guidance and there was not one in the crowd who wasn't special, gifted or talented in some way. These were daughters and sons of someone, parents and friends, very good people with good hearts. I took my being there seriously and "side" counseled some as they asked, sometimes without words, hearing stories of how and why they were there.

One young girl in particular stayed on my mind because at that point she had not attended any classes whatsoever or as far as I knew hadn't left her room. I just had a quick glance occasionally as I walked by, if her door was cracked open, and I kept realizing she must be so lonely or depressed or just scared, maybe all of those things. I will admit she was quite attractive. One evening as time was getting late I went to smoke a cig and there she was, smoking also, looking away and down like a frightened deer and wanting to be invisible. Somehow we just quietly began speaking and I gave her all the personal and private space I could, not trying to draw any conversation out, just letting things progress at her speed, if at all. The talk began as it should have, simple subjects like music, food, life in general. If she felt comfortable enough to go deeper so be it, I was in her eyes in the same boat as herself and not a preacher.

The next day she joined us for breakfast, still very quiet and private, and afterwards we just began sharing a little here and there. In very short time we were joking and laughing, taking walks around the block and ordering pizza late night. She was from a well to do out of state family having yachts, 4 story beach houses and the like, implanted from far away so as not to be an embarrassment to the family, insecure and out of place to be sure. She had opened up and come out of her shell to me simply because I noticed and paid attention, and just let her be herself on her time....it was extremely rewarding to me as well, because I saw dark turn to light. The thought of the wealth she had come from, the need for her loved ones to ship her off to nowhere, not for her benefit but so they could continue their picture perfect lifestyle. She told me there was a celebratory yacht trip planned for her, as she was nearing the completion of soberness. They had no idea she had only attended maybe 4 classes out of 60 or so. What she needed was an ear, patience and a little compassion. I really do feel good about getting her to open up and share some walks and laughs. Had she wanted to share other things of course I likely would have obliged. I sometimes do wonder if she ever thinks of it.

From my private meetings with her on I would be called to the reception area a few times to meet new people, put them at ease, comfort nervous parents and show them around, trying to assure them their kid would be safe. It was a truly warming feeling when a mother and father left their young son with me, they had arrived only moments before. The kid had a look of bewilderment and concern which passed on to the parents. I assured them he would be fine, no trouble would come to him. I did sincerely mean it. There had been scuffles at times, occasionally police were called. When a mother, tears running down her face, passes her child off to another it's a bit overwhelming. The father had teared up also and I could feel myself not too far behind. The feeling that day was something I can't put into words. It was the sense of having some purpose not only for the kid but the parents as well. I was blessed by their being there and they would never know it. I do enjoy the thought that as they returned to regular life they had at least some sense of peace. I was asked at one point later to actually lead one of the evening classes but I declined thinking I didn't come here to work!! Honestly I didn't feel like I was in the best position to do so for various reasons.

On my last day there were lots of hugs and some tears, phone numbers exchanged. I was vindicated in knowing I could turn away with the proper help and the feeling that others were like me helped much as well. I got to my car and settled in, then an overwhelming sense of doom. What was I going to do now? The home life and situations were not going to be friendly to my needs, the 30 day treatment really had not addressed any underlying causes. Within a half hour I knew I was in trouble. I had to return to my only existence, there was no choice. I stopped at the first available ABC store and went right back to the place in my head I had conquered 30 days ago. The shame and guilt were overwhelming, crushing really. I had to tell myself that I'm not a demon, not a monster, some people do in fact care about me. This is who I am, this is what I do, accept it or not. Within 2 weeks I heard that one of my friends at that facility, having been released, died within days of leaving. He apparently went on a binge and took it too far.

When I returned to normal life and some time had passed I received several texts and emails asking me to consider mentoring young adults or people otherwise on the wrong path. I did consider it but the calling wasn't there. I know that in any given event I could have been accused of a sexual assault or anything of that nature had someone just not cared for something I said. Given the age difference and a bit of my past it wasn't worth the risk. I also knew in my heart that should I attempt it I would have had too much empathy for them, especially being young. That empathy would likely not work well with my being open and forthright completely, as in not wanting to hurt any feelings. If I had made someone cry or feel shamed game over, because then I would also. I do believe however that I could have been somewhat good at it had it not been for the empathy-caring-human part. How and why I got those messages is unknown, as well as where from. It opened my eyes a little in any event, I really could help others according to some.

Throughout the many years of craziness I was fortunate to not be caught with any substances, the opportunity was certainly there at times. Times like 3:00, 5:30, 7:00 am. Personally I knew and had partied with active duty officers a few times, good people who just didn't like the job anymore. Very good to have on your side in any event. I never disliked police but didn't trust in them either. I had seen several female officers who got my attention for sure. At one outdoor community gathering a very attractive lady nicely asked as we moved about if I had any weapons, things of that nature, which I did not. Thinking quickly, hoping for a good outcome I replied "I can't remember." I had the brilliant idea that having said that she might want to give me a good pat down. There was no animosity, I wasn't being a smartass, rather a dumbass. Now the stage was set for that frisk, yet it came from her male coworker dammit. She was sly and not ignorant to my ignorance. I deserve a little credit for that effort though!

In the end what was verified to me through the professionals, which I already knew was that everyone has an addiction. Every person 10 years or older has an addiction of some sort assuming their cognitive abilities are intact. Something else occurred to me also, having seen those seeking help and those needing but not seeking. It doesn't matter who, rich or poor, known or invisible, everyone has at one time or another made a choice or decision that was not correct for one reason or another. I'm going to take that a bit further and say 100% have made more than just one by far. We look at others and their deeds and criticize with disbelief thinking how awful, how could someone do such? I know I've been guilty of it. That judgement is a way for people to justify their own doings by comparison. It makes one feel sanctified to think 'yes I did this thing and that but I didn't do what he or she did.'

I'm not speaking of violent crime and that sort of thing but more of lifestyles and behavior one wouldn't tell their grandmother about. In conclusion, wherever you travel or even just looking out of the window, any person you see has made a few mistakes, not always been right. That person you see, everyone they know, everyone you know and anyone you've ever passed in a store or on a highway. If everyone were to stop judging, stop criticizing and focus on their own imperfections I believe life would get so much better all around. I'm going to start myself by approaching my neighbor even if he is an asshole jerkoff. Kidding, just kidding, not really a "neighbor" but in the immediate area. Still an ass.

An addiction in brief terms is a chronic mental issue sometimes driven by genetics, perhaps an environment or life experiences, certainly there are other factors. There are addictions to the obvious, drugs and alcohol, which are shunned and very highly misunderstood by most. Less well known, unspoken addictions could be physical fitness, social media, sex, clothing attire, sports, appearance, gaming, success, food, dozens more, and the deadliest of all, religion. Any category, faith or denomination on any continent, throughout human history.

How did all those days, nights, years treat me? Let me say this, between my cohorts and I the laughter and snickering was misunderstood and unmatched by many, in some cases probably approaching arrogance. It's almost like the perfect storm of clowns miraculously ended up in a predestined area and as with other storms, causing at the least some concern or in drastic cases some decided to pack up and move. If that be true the plan was perfection. We didn't always get away with things. The speeches of immorality and illegality were just expected, usually not taken seriously. We lived while we were alive so to speak, and there were activities I know other people envisioned and wished they could've done themselves. There are also many regrets and scars, shame as well. I had seen people shot, cut, overdose, lose possessions and loved ones, wail and cry, so many painful things. Seeing grown men cry, even if it was warranted in some way is unbearable. I say that because the men I speak of were the toughest around and had been in many tough spots. The crying from an observers point of view was not about tears but pain that had not yet been acknowledged, and now it's exceedingly painful. Some may say they had it coming, maybe so. Whether they did or didn't makes it no easier to watch or here, those angry emotions releasing after years. It really pained me also to see some that I loved fall so hard over time, losing so much. I would be beckoned at times to visit or help someone in some way and the visual upon entering where they now call home was shocking. Bottles covering every inch of anything flat, cans, discarded food and wrappers, clothing, full trash bags. At one location the mice were actually unafraid, unconcerned about the presence of people. I thought I saw a little mouse reclined on some old throw pillow, on his back with one little arm behind his head, the other scratching his belly. Legs crossed, yawning and picking his teeth with his tongue.

I had witnessed beat downs, arrests and so on. In most cases the authorities were doing what they were supposed to and I harbor no bad feelings, I'm pro blue all the way. Years ago I had wandered into a field heading for the trees after a physical confrontation, just trying to get away without direction. In very little time police were everywhere but unaware of my precise location. I heard one officer say "bring the dogs" which needless to say got my attention. I came out so fast they probably thought my ass was on fire. My point being they did their job, no hard feelings. I was vindicated when all was said and done concerning that event, no charges or issues.

I had likewise met with some rich and famous folks from the NFL, Nascar, a few musical well knowns and a couple from Hollywood. To better say it the good, the bad & the ugly. I was never star struck because I knew they were nothing more than people. Much higher salaries than most but in the end, we are all equal in the grave. Six feet of dirt recognizes no one. Speaking of which someone asked me what might be on my tombstone on that tombstone day. Probably something like my last known words, which might have been..."hey, watch this!!" My tombstone, at that point announcing my demise reminds me of another asking what would God think of your existence, what might he say? That's very thought provoking. I can relay what I'd like to hear, not that it would transpire but possible. Something along the lines of..."My son, you've been through much and faltered many times. Why did you not lean on faith and call to me as I had made available to you? Despite these things you are forgiven, your battle is over, welcome."

The truth is the more time that went by the worse things became. I considered suicide more than once, to the point of gripping my handgun, pressed firmly against my head and a flash came to me, put it down. I also thought of my mom and how it would affect her, additionally the awful mess it would leave behind for others. I'm so damn empathetic I can't even kill myself. I then went to pharmaceuticals, much less of a mess, and ingested no telling how many of who knows what, narcotics is all I know. It didn't work as planned and I ended up in some hospital wing dedicated for persons who may be a danger to others or themselves. I can only surmise it wasn't quite my time.

I was angry, embarrassed and without care for pretty much anything. So many people crying, asking "what did you do? WHY? WHY? WHY?" How is one supposed to answer that? I didn't give much thought to those who might have cared. In the moment you're getting ready to end it the last thought is the feelings of others, you just want the pain to end. To that point I've heard people say more than once that suicide is the easy way out. Having been there myself, as well as talking with others in that situation,

I'll stand firm saying it's not easy at all, far from it. It takes a person quite a bit of fortitude to carry through, especially when they're crying their eyes out and begging for forgiveness for something yet to come. Some people are perfectly mentally fit, just don't give a damn anymore. Those two episodes were years ago and I can assume I'm still here for some reason. That being said I have very much had those same thoughts since, many times. The direction I was always pointed in without fail was doctors and pills, over and over again. Seems to be the antidote for any and all of lifes' ills. Certainly that's what the doctors and pharmaceutical industry want once they get any insurance information. Is that not always question one? "Hey I'm in a lot of pain and thinking about just ending it all." "Yes sir, and what type of insurance do you have?"

The space between those who love their lives and those willing to end their own is blurred somewhat. There seems to be a crossroad where empathy meets compassion, therein lies the problem. From my teen years on I became more lenient with many things which fosters compassion on a larger scale. Many times I felt compassion for my involvement in any manner where someone was hurt either physically or verbally, so I continued to evolve in that sense. At the same time I would be more empathetic in regard to people I did not know, never met, something one see on the news for example. For myself empathy was more of a heartache, compassion was more of an understanding sometimes mixed with anger for whatever happened. In either case I was realizing things, learning.

Compassion is something largely taught by our parents or elders, passed down and passed on throughout generations. Compassion has unwritten rules, we just believe what we know to be right as we have seen others show compassion in whatever circumstance. There is a high degree of morality within compassion, morality has always been defined by man and to a large extent religion. In other words compassion is what we say it is.

Empathy is something inherent, born into living beings as with a soul. I believe it can be manipulated to some degree but still remains. There are countless documentaries where elephants in the wild trek to elephant graveyards, as the reference goes. They visit those sites multiple times throughout their lives, showing the younger ones how to get there. Once they arrive they begin to touch, feel, gently rub the bones and tusks of the deceased and moan or wail. Their eyes show such care and some sense of loss, truly an amazing sight. That is the very definition of empathy, clearly inbred long ago. Likewise I watched as an entire herd crossed a very large river going completely under water for some time until they reached the opposite bank. There was one little baby elephant left behind, too scared to venture into the water, the others now far away. To my amazement the herd reversed course, every single one of them and returned for the one left behind. That is more than some humans would do, no question. Does that action show compassion or empathy?

We unfortunately are forced at times to end the life of an animal knowing the only other option would be prolonged misery. A horse with a terribly broken leg, a hunting dog barely hanging on after being gutted by a wild boar. We make the decision to end their pain and yes we suffer because of it. Concerning human beings however we suddenly become more selective and care not an ounce about the actual person in question. My true meaning is simple, if a person known or unknown was suffering from some affliction that caused never ending pain and suffering and just wanted the pain to end, by their own hand or choice, suddenly morals enter. People who never met that person, knew nothing of their plight, never felt their actual pain or previously gave a damn about them suddenly appear claiming their view of right is right. Those same people, with a heavy heart, said yes to putting an animal out of misery the day before.

It doesn't matter if someone has a disorder whereby they feel like their skin is on fire constantly, just put them in a special room while we take 6 years to address it, we should have the thoughts of doctors, theologists and scientists. All the while that horse had been thankfully freed from suffering as it should have been. I do not believe suicide is something that anyone should consider whatsoever, hell thinking of my own demise almost killed me before the actual attempt. When unending pain that cannot be rectified or even diminished enters the picture and someone says please end it, that's another story. If humans could actually walk a mile in someone else's shoes as the saying goes, my guess is most would take 2 steps, complain about the fit, maybe say something doesn't feel right or whatever, then return those same shoes with comforters inserted, problem solved.

Having said that my point is for those who feel like they want to end it all for whatever reason, the last thing I would say to them is "you need counseling" or "I understand" and then walk away shaking your head. Another response, far worse is "how could you do that to me"? A response like that just shifted the attention to the one who spoke it and also piled more weight onto the other. For those who have to deal with another that may have attempted suicide, my suggestion is true empathy. Listen, hear, decipher the words and apply a large amount of common sense, not bewilderment. If you not only hear but more importantly listen, in a lot of cases the words they speak are not what they are truly saying, although the meaning is there. Some express things the only way they know, words can hide the meaning. I sincerely wish that no one ever finds themselves in either situation.

On a few unfortunate occasions I was side by side with someone slowly passing, holding their hand or just touching somehow so they knew they were not alone. I witnessed that last breath and the letting go more than once. It obviously hurt personally but the ones in question surrendered without a struggle or crying, in those cases any struggle would've been pointless. I don't know how to describe or explain but I was almost envious. I had seen death yes, however I had also seen those who died many deaths yet still among us.

Some may have seen a drowning person calling for help and just passed by. At a later time that person found out things did not have to be that way, if only someone had given 20 seconds or so. Another may have withheld things that could have, would have saved another. They still possess whatever it was, though it is of no value now. The value disappeared along with the one who could have been saved. Clearly analogies, but stories lie behind them. Those who held back for no good reason died every day after the fact, slowly and did so until death.

In retrospect my very early years were somewhat split between confusion, distrust and having been exposed to things inappropriate for someone in that age group. I did participate in things on my own surely, right or wrong. I do wonder how things might have been were those situations not presented to me, meaning I would have been unaware of some things at least until a later time. Maybe things do happen for a specific reason.

In my early teens I had managed to scrape together some semblance of maturity. I held on to some of my beliefs and discarded others, or at least partially forgot. At the latter teen stage and onward I had been reinvented and happily so. That being said I overcame the foolish desires of a punk kid and replaced them with more adult desires just as crazy but having worse consequences. I suppose it makes sense that the older one gets the bigger the risks, the bigger the laughs at times.

I had clearly embraced education and learned to present myself to others respectfully in terms of conversation and appearance. The biggest factor was respect for others, being mannerly and polite and simply applying the golden rule. No more illegal entries or borrowing vehicles without permission, no shoplifting etc. Those ugly habits were easily buried by choosing the right people to associate with and turning away from the ones that participated in the cycle of keeping each other down. That is to say those who actively continue to do so. Bye.

STAGE 3

So here I am now all these crazy years later, occasionally wondering why and how I made it this far. The events and activities portrayed are indeed true, those things happened. For every story and lurid detail expressed 50 have been left out. I didn't want this manuscript to turn into something the size of a dictionary. Very infrequently I look back at photographs and other items I held on to that bring things back to me. Some of the things I've done I simply feel indifferent to, only a few things bring any joy, the majority bring nothing but shame, guilt and depression. Some might think "what a crazy fun party life..." I do know from word of mouth others at times thought I had it all in those younger years. First of all, what is "it"? I did have the greatest of times in a period, the best friends one could ask for, a family life and certain abilities. Those things are gone now, most importantly the people. What I have now is memories, half of which are a curse. When anyone says "had it all", well compared to who? Had is a past tense word anyway, meaning no longer. It's all part of the cycle we call life.

The years of living like a fool destroyed me physically and a little mentally. My body is beaten from the constant drumming, partying and living large. Getting around these days is a chore occasionally but I have no complaints considering others have things in their lives much worse. It's not attributed to aging solely but mostly to poor decisions and such, to which health professionals do agree. My hands for example have become shaky, unreliable at times due to the never ending stress of the constant grip and usage they received over time with the bands. Shoulders, back, same thing. Pain medicine and aspirin have become necessary intakes and make little difference.

Another issue was an internal health scare I was unaware of briefly. I had a stroke in my sleep one evening that was not detected until the following day when I noticed significant vision loss in one eye. Eventually I went from the ER to cat-scans to other specialists and such, the verdict was clear. I will say that it didn't seem to be a life or death situation at the time but when the word "stroke" becomes part of the dialogue it does grab attention quickly.

The more powerful realization has been mental, coming to terms with things I've done. Clearly I had troubles in some environments I was placed in or had placed myself in. In large part any physical altercations I was involved in were defensive, I did not seek those things out. I had said to one I trusted that I probably wouldn't live to see 50 considering the sabotage of clean living, but the powers that be had other plans, a blessing. My mother raised me knowing full well right from wrong but I ignored the teachings that would have prevented me from participating in things that tempted me too strongly.

Considering the few entries of ignorance and apparent lack of care I've submitted this may sound strange. I have always had the strongest empathy, concern or caring for others. Yes I took without asking and spoke without thinking, I did indeed cause a bit of pain otherwise. Those things bothered me and haunted me endlessly, some still. Why I continued to do so in my earlier years I can't say. As I aged and became more aware I wanted so much to be an equalizer of sorts, one to make things right or right those who were wronged. I have acted on that thought a few times in terms of giving something I couldn't really afford to give or offering some sort of assistance whether I had the means or not. The feeling for me was a warmth of sorts, and it was made more so due to the fact those people were complete strangers, in some store or venue, and I knew we'd never see each other again.

On one occasion I had heard of several different people known to me that had fallen on really hard times. Known to me but vaguely. I did a little research to pinpoint their homes and began to gather what funds and such I could. They had not reached out themselves, others had mentioned their troubles in passing. I was able to deliver certain pre-paid cards from various places to them in complete privacy, driving to their location and putting them directly into their mailboxes, no one knowing but myself. After a few days I would see where people had posted on certain sites what they had heard, the gratitude of the recipients, saying what an overwhelming relief and blessing it had been. Well, I had been blessed myself to be in a position to do it.

I never spoke of it, it remains a mystery to them as it should. One should not freely give only to turn and say "look what I did." Those things are not meant for self-glorification, that itself diminishes the true thought of giving. I say it now because I am unknown by choice, those who received are unknown as well. Hopefully some will read this and maybe improve on my efforts in one way or another to see, recognize a need and act on it, privately. If it involves a complete stranger all the better. Upon my word you will feel your soul light up. My gifting does not in any way diminish my past, the two are not related. If it makes me feel a little better on a personal level I'll take it, privately, and others can benefit.

The overall view of my behavior is painful and sobering. I had stolen, fought for things not worthy of fighting for, physically hurt people as well as causing undo mental stress and anguish to who knows how many. All of those things pale in comparison to me knowing I had committed adultery, more than once. That whole temptation and free will thing beat me pretty good. The wife and I were faithful ourselves, a couple of our partners though were indeed married. That pain is one that cannot be written down or verbalized, it just hurts throughout and I suppose deservedly so. My conscience had been treated like a doormat so much it had become unheard but never gave up. The fact is I did care about many things and hurt for many people throughout, I guess I convinced myself otherwise or drank it away.

If comparing ying and yang mathematically I'd say the fun outnumbered the bad times but the bad times were much more pronounced. Myself and my motley associates had pulled through tough spots and seen much, with the exception of a few who aren't with us anymore. In short we lived despite the carelessness. Then there are many others who later in life wonder what might have been. As the Quiet One said once, "Life goes on within you and without you". Indeed it does.

When I began to document these things several years ago I had certainly slowed down a little, making room for the next generation I suppose. Sadly before I even got a decent start my wife passed away and nothing has been even remotely the same. We had been together for so long and been through so much, both good and bad. Very soon afterwards I began to actually see how everything had changed. She knew of my writing and encouraged it, even making suggestions at times which has given me the will to just do it.

If nothing else comes of the things I've shared, please do take the following to heart. During our last few years together we had argued quite a bit as some long term couples do. Not an all day, everyday thing but not far from it. The disagreements were stupid, nothing of real importance. We both knew how to argue on a professional level and did just that, neither willing to concede most times. We did love each other, we just were not in love at the end. When she passed, that's how she left this world and that's how I was left in it. There was no hugging, no I'm sorry, no I love you, and it was too late. I can say without a doubt that having that with me now is truly a cancer that eats at me constantly. I feel like I will never get over it completely and that's a very heavy load. Neither of us had done anything truly unforgiveable, not remotely. It just came to bickering about anything and everything, habitual really. Please, if it's within your power, do not go to bed angry or put off offering an olive branch to a loved one, as I type this now I can say with all confidence it's not worth it to be angry or hard headed. One day, any given day, will be the last time you see or speak to that someone, that much I can guarantee.

There were many friends and/or colleagues that were nowhere to be found after her passing, the same goes for some actual family. To their credit most had given certain things up, developed a respectable lifestyle and simply moved on. What a grand idea, if only I had considered it earlier.

This entire opening up exercise would be pointless for myself if I had not held my head up to a degree and exposed truths and episodes whether they were painful or shameful or the opposite. Keeping with that format I really feel as if I need to shed something else.

When the wife passed there was much sympathy, hugging and storytelling from some of our longtime friends, of course some family as well. That type of support is truly welcome and needed in the quick aftermath of a passing.

On the evening of her actual service there were many in attendance as expected. There was also a glaring absence of more than a few that initially in my mind would absolutely make an appearance. I am speaking of several that were like brothers and sisters for decades, those who were much closer than most and had shared much more. I didn't give it any thought for a day or two, certainly not that night, but it began to eat at me.

I knew those in question were still close by and had heard the news, there's no question. Likewise I was told of 1 or 2 that had certain health issues that just didn't permit them to come, I understand that completely and had no hard feelings whatsoever. As for the remaining no-shows, it's different because I knew of their circumstances and such.

There were 3 or 4 that not so much as sent a text or card, no phone calls, no dropping by, nothing. People that had been my extended family for over 30 years and in some cases knew the wife before me. In their hour of need the wife, myself or at times both made it a priority to be there. People do change and move on in life, that for some is or was well overdue. I'll just say this and be done, they can't say they didn't know, can't say there wasn't enough time to text a 6 or 7 word sentence. What they can say is "it's no big deal, wasn't my wife, I'm too busy". I'm glad some transformed from a creepy crawly into a butterfly, but it was not a complete transformation.

Just too quickly finish that topic off there are some I run into occasionally at a store or just in passing that were likewise very close but somewhere along the line had been convinced that they were beyond reproach. When I would see them it was so painfully clear they were uncomfortable and I knew without any doubt one of the following phrases would be uttered...

"I was just thinking about you!" or "I was getting ready to call you" or "we need to have you over for dinner" and lastly "let's get together for a drink or something" I was correct each time, one of those phrases, sometimes two, every single time. Being the not so politically correct one I am, allow me to say just stop please, lying to someone directly in that circumstance is not an attribute. Remember, I know you! I would very much appreciate the kind words or invites IF they were sincere. As a great man once said, when you know, assuredly, that someone is lying allow them to keep lying and believing it was successful. Eventually they are painted into a corner that another lie cannot cover. The ones in question know better anyway, so there still remains a little animosity on my end. If one were to call needing something however, I would oblige.

I truly, honestly wish the nicer things in life on those who really want that change and make it happen as long as it's done the right way. When others are stepped on or the like as a means to change, well life is a cycle and comes back around. If and when the past catches up with them, all they need do is reach out, I won't ignore.

There were some that passed on for various reasons as my wife had, and reality sets in at a slow pace. I'm solitary now, something new to me as I have never been so. My being in that new arena doesn't really work well and honestly I have been basically an empty shell for some time. Aimless, lost, no direction whatsoever and mostly not even knowing the day or at times even the month. I do realize that many other lives are much worse without a doubt, thing is I'm not dwelling on others at this time, only trying to figure out my hour by hour existence and questioning how to proceed. Things do happen for reasons, I do believe that. If an occasion turns up and it becomes noticeable that someone is exhibiting the habits and things documented here, reach out if it's in your nature to do so. You may not have any answers to certain things but you can now speak on consequences. Know your limitations, know your friends and acquaintances, ask yourself "what if..." in any unsure circumstance. I failed at least partially with all three.

I offer all apologies to those I may have offended, hurt, disrespected, steered wrong, taken from or anything likewise. I do have to try to move on and I hope others can also. Is it actually possible for me to do so, change, reinvent myself, and act like a normal person? Will I ever meet someone special again? In my mind right now, no. I really really hope to be wrong on those thoughts but there is that undeniable thing called reality.

I cannot guarantee every bit of foolishness has been exhausted!

STAGE 4

?

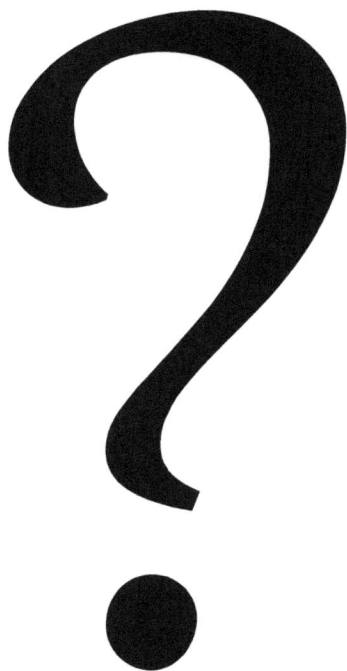

www.ingramcontent.com/pod-product-compliance
Lightning Source LLC
Chambersburg PA
CBHW051834040426
42447CB00006B/516
9798892855792